A FUNNY THING HAPPENED ON THE WAY TO HEAVEN

ALSO BY COREY TAYLOR

Seven Deadly Sins

COREY TAYLOR

A FUNNY THING HAPPENED ON THE WAY TO HEAVEN

(OR, HOW I MADE PEACE WITH THE PARANORMAL
AND STIGMATIZED ZEALOTS AND CYNICS
IN THE PROCESS)

EBURY
PRESS

1 3 5 7 9 10 8 6 4 2

First published in 2013 by Ebury Press, an imprint of Ebury Publishing
A Random House Group company
Published in the USA by Da Capo Press,
a member of the Perseus Book Group in 2013

The Random House Group Limited Reg. No. 954009

Addresses for companies within the Random House Group can be found at
www.randomhouse.co.uk

A CIP catalogue record for this book is available from the British Library

The Random House Group Limited supports the Forest Stewardship Council® (FSC®),
the leading international forest-certification organisation. Our books carrying the
FSC label are printed on FSC®-certified paper. FSC is the only forest-certification
scheme supported by the leading environmental organisations, including Greenpeace.
Our paper procurement policy can be found at www.randomhouse.co.uk/environment

MIX
Paper from
responsible sources
FSC® C016897

Printed and bound by CPI Group (UK) Ltd, Croydon, CR0 4YY

HB ISBN 9780091949655
TPB ISBN 9780091957001

To buy books by your favourite authors and register for offers visit
www.randomhouse.co.uk

This book is dedicated as always to my family,
who keep me focused and inspired on an almost infinite loop.
Without them, I am ever the rambler.
With them, I am always ready, willing, and aware.
I love you all with every bit of my heart.

Also, I dedicate this to Charles Bonnici,
who taught me more about devotion, love,
and what it means to be a man than
any other living being on earth.
I miss you, Dad.
And I'll do my best.

contents

At first cock-crow the ghosts must go
Back to their quiet graves below.
  —Theodosia Garrison

There was something awesome in the thought of the solitary
mortal standing by the open window and summoning in
from the gloom outside the spirits of the nether world.
  —Sir Arthur Conan Doyle

I don't know if God exists, but it would be better for
His reputation if He didn't.
  —Jules Renard

What is this that stands before me?
Figure in black which points at me.
  —John "Ozzy" Osbourne, "Black Sabbath," Black Sabbath

A FUNNY THING HAPPENED ON THE WAY TO HEAVEN

COLD HOUSE

YOU SEE THEM EVERYWHERE THESE DAYS. You see them in movies and cartoons, advertisements and reality shows. Celebrities line up to tell their stories just so they have a good excuse to shiver and shake in their designer sports jackets. They are so common today that it is almost crazy to imagine a time when the very idea was disturbing. But there was indeed an era when the thought of ghosts was enough to send a tendril of chilly dread down your spine. I am not talking about the guy under the sheet with the eyeholes cut out or the "groovy" spooks that have been plaguing Scooby and the gang since 1969. I am talking about the footsteps right behind you, the padded shuffle on hardwood floors where there should be no noise at all. I am talking about the shadow in the corner of your eye when you are sitting at home alone. I am talking about moving objects and flying silverware and waking up with scratches you know for a fact were not there when you went to bed. There are spaces between spaces and doors that go nowhere. From orbs to shades, the spirit end of the paranormal pool is anything but shallow, but it is easy to find yourself drowning.

When you are young, if you are anywhere near a group of same-aged folk and you want to freak each other out, you tell ghost stories. You gather up a blanket and you swap them like baseball cards at the expo, waiting with your breath held for your turn at the mike because, nine times out of ten, everyone in that room has a ghost story. They can be as vanilla as seeing your great grandfather in the cellar or they can be as mollifying as the dark shape that follows you to every town you have lived in since you were still taking naps in school. But in my experience almost everyone I know has a ghost story, and anyone who does not have one secretly and desperately wants one.

People have been infatuated with the supernatural almost as long as they have been with religion. In fact, if religion were a lounge singer, then the paranormal would be a rock star. Unless you worship snakes or speak in tongues, most of the time your chosen faith is fairly banal. But the unexplained . . . shit, that is like your first leather jacket or your first French kiss. Taboo is always the more appealing possibility. Maybe it is the implied darkness or the fantasy side, but I do know ghost stories are more intriguing because no two are really the same. The Bible only really changes when someone new comes to power.

And let's face facts: people love being scared. It is the same reason I watch every damn shark movie that comes out, even though the mere sight of them makes me want to fill my pants with the brown sound—I love the feeling. You do not take a first date to a chick flick; you take her to something that is going to make her jump straight into your arms in terror, preferably at a drive-in. Nothing too gross and gory—something that is just intense enough to close the deal for you. Ghost stories are quite simply our early introduction into that fierce side of the world. It is bonding and sharing and fucking with people all rolled into one. It is delicious masochism.

I am about to tell you a story that I have not recounted to anyone since I was fourteen years old. It is extraordinary, terrifying, and, at the risk of committing the sin of pun, very haunting. It is also true; some of the events are a bit loose, as this happened to me thirty years ago, but the pieces I remember are as vibrant today as the night they occurred, and the more I write it down, the more it is all coming back to me—stronger, clearer, and more defined. Doubt if you want. Scoff if you wish. It does not change the fact that *it happened*. And I was there. For better or worse, I was there.

I was nine years old in the summer of 1983, "growing up" on the south side of Des Moines, Iowa, my hometown backdrop off and on for most of my life. Unbeknownst to me, I was a year away from moving to Florida and spending the better part of my teens on the move, forever giving up any semblance of roots in favor of a second-rate vagabond existence. But in '83 I had been in Des Moines for three wonderful years and had managed to find some semblance of a real life, to feel like a real kid. I was a Cub Scout until an unfortunate brake failure caused me to ride my BMX through the screen door of my scoutmaster's house. I played little league baseball and bowled on a kids' league (on a team that was *meant* to be called "The Cannibals," but some adult renamed us "The Cannon Ballers" . . .) at a beautiful old alley called Bowlerama, where my grandmother had bowled since before I was born. I lived in a basement apartment just a short walk away from the corner of South East 14th and Watrous Avenue, and from first to mid-fourth grade I attended Andrew Jackson Elementary School, which was only a few blocks away. You could follow Watrous right to Jackson's front door if you wanted, wind around the corner-hook that finally t-boned at Indianola Avenue, then cross the school's vast front yard. But there was another more direct and mysterious route that led you to the school, opening out onto its parking lot and the outside playground.

Before the convenience store moved years later, the Quik-Trip gas station on 14th and Watrous was on the other side of the street. Perpendicular to the shop was nothing but forest, only really cut off by the houses that lined the way to school. But there was a path through the woods that was very nearly a straight line to Jackson Elementary. So my friends and I would sidestep the street, make our way through the trees, and head deep into what we called the South Side Woods. The path itself twisted and turned, providing a virtually crazy maze that we happily skipped on as the morning dew dried under a warm morning sun. But as we got closer to school, the woods took on a fairly sinister feeling.

About halfway through the expanse, bizarre "traps" and gnarly rusted tripwires started popping up on the path. They were specifically designed to fuck with anyone on the path itself—the wires crossed it like someone was trying to catch us and hurt us. Knowing the trail as well as we did, we still had to watch where we were going. The strange thing was that every once in a while the wires and traps would move—someone was moving them. We never knew why. However, as dangerous as these hazards were for a bunch of kids, what lay up ahead was like something out of a Wes Craven movie.

In the middle of this forest, clearly removed from the community that surrounded it, stood a two-story abandoned house, gutted and decrepit, a tower of foreboding set against this suburban gothic landscape like a hangover from the Brothers Grimm's seedier days. It was the essence of the color gray and defiant in the face of the elements; no one really knew how old it was, how long it had been there, or who had wanted to live there, seeing as it was not on any street nor did it have a driveway that connected it to the outside world. It was just a hulking mess that scared the ever-living shit out of us kids—terrifying messages had been scrawled on the outside walls, most likely by teenagers who hung out there. Thinking back now, it was really just a creepy house that creaked and shuddered, but to impressionable nine-year-olds, it was the vacation spot of the devil itself. Of course we were fascinated by it even as we avoided it like the plague. But none of us had the stones to go in. Even on a dare—

which to a kid is like a binding contract you could take to court—we would not go near it. We hurried past as much to get away from it as we did to get to school on time. But even when we could not see it, we knew it was there, and we talked about it constantly, so much so that my friends and I started referring to it as Cold House.

The summer of '83 was a huge time in my life. I was beginning to think a lot like I do today, and I was starting to realize that kids liked spending time with me because I had no fear and was constantly entertaining. After *Return of the Jedi* came out, my friends and I would recreate the movie, and I was always voted Luke Skywalker, charging onto the field we usually played stickball on with my broken secondhand plastic red lightsaber to save the day. I rolled with a lot of neighborhood kids, some the same age and some a little older. You could find us at my house after school—watching *G.I. Joe* cartoons on WGN and videos on a newer station called MTV because we were one of the few families who actually had cable, albeit stolen. So I always had friends around, and during that summer there was always a sleepover at someone's house.

It was July when my friends and I decided to sneak out of my apartment and go explore Cold House.

There were six of us: I was basically the ringleader, and then there was my first real best friend, Henry, along with Matt, Joe, Tina, and Brock. Henry and Matt lived a few blocks away and were the only ones technically staying overnight with me. Joe, Tina, and Brock lived in other buildings in the complex. The plan came together earlier that day while we were roaming around looking for shit to do. When kids are starving in the brain, their heads seek out mischievous fun. There is the old adage "idle hands are the devil's playthings." No truer words have ever been said: I almost got my family evicted from that apartment complex because I broke into one of the storage garages—and by "break in" I mean I went through the wall with a used iron bar.

For a long time I had wanted to go into Cold House and see what was there. We had heard it was haunted since we had first started taking the trails to school. The thought of a potentially real haunted house not two blocks away from where I slept was too much for me to contemplate, and I was bound and determined to get inside and see what I could see. My cohorts were of course a bit more reticent than I was. Tina did not want to have anything to do with it; the others only wanted to go during the day. I wanted to go at night, possessed by the idea that the only time we would see anything was after midnight. No one had to go who did not wish to—this was "Join Us at Your Own Risk." Finally we found ourselves on the same scary page and went to work.

The plan was this: we would meet behind the work shed near my building at 12 A.M. Henry, Matt, and I would sneak out of my bedroom window, which I had done countless times before. The rest would find a way to get there, if they were indeed going to come along. Tina, Joe, and Brock still hummed and hawed at the idea, but at midnight, when my group was safely behind the shed, the other three soon met us and we were on our way. We had managed to smuggle four flashlights into our bedrooms that day. We walked down 14th, crossed at the lights, and, making sure to keep out of sight of adults who might try to send us back home, proceeded into the South Side Woods, waving the flashlights around like Jedis to keep the jitters at bay.

Before we go any further, let me tell you first that, as always, I have changed my friends' names out of respect to what happened and because, even though I have not seen them since shortly after this incident, they will forever be tied to me as friends and as people who got through this unscathed. I doubt they would even admit remembering this night if pressed. But my profession has a way of keeping youthful exuberance fresh and, therefore, my recollection of the following events are as vivid as yesterday. So this is my book, my obsession, and my quandary; to call them out would mean making them question shit from the past they have probably done their best to forget. Make no mistake though: these are actual events; I was not by myself, and I have the scars to prove it.

The six of us found ourselves fairly jovial, even though we were traipsing through the darkness toward something that frightened us to death. Even when we tripped on the wires draped over the path, we laughed and helped each other up. We kept moving, each of us certain we were going to see something "so fucking cool!" Then, before we knew it and a lot sooner than we expected, we were there.

I cannot tell you how much more terrifying Cold House looked in the dark. Years later, watching the end of *Blair Witch Project*, I experienced a horrendous and violent flashback. I felt petrified because it took me directly back to that night. It was like someone had been with us filming. Of course that was a movie designed to make you piss your pants and give you motion sickness—memory and reality can be so much more vicious.

Casting our flashlights across its dilapidated façade, it had the appearance of a killer. It was like discovering an alligator in the water next to you. All of the windows were gone of course, targets for teens throwing rocks and those hard green things that smelled like Pine-Sol that fell from the trees everywhere. In fact, the trees around the house looked like ghoulish fingers, either holding it in place or pointing at us, the interlopers, seeming to tell us to keep away. The front door hung on one hinge at an awful angle, and the steps up onto the front porch looked so weak that even Indiana Jones would have found another way inside. We all stood there, kind of frozen in excitement and fear. Were we really going to fucking *do* this? It seemed like I was the only one ready and willing to make this happen. With a fire I still cannot describe or explain from whence it came, I left the path and took four steps toward the house—the closest I had ever come to going inside in my life. My legs were rubber and my heart was threatening to escape from my chest, but I moved even closer. The sound of feet sliding through tall grass let me know my comrades were following, although not too closely.

I moved cautiously on the porch steps. Each one that took my weight complained loudly, and even though there was city noise not too far away, in the dark and silence of the woods, those creaking sounds were like needles sliding across your ears. We might as well have been in Romania—home seemed a million miles away. The porch itself was a little more stable, and we gathered there before I reached out with inactive fingers to move the front door and gain access to Cold House. One by one, we crossed its threshold.

Then all our flashlights went dead.

Studying the paranormal as I have over the years, I have read about spirits draining batteries and power sources for the energy to manifest. I found this to be true when, in 2003 and part of 2004, I experienced similar activity at the fabled mansion on Laurel Canyon in Los Angeles. But we will talk about that later. Back in 1983 I did not know about this phenomenon. I was just a nine-year-old kid suddenly plunged into pitch black in an abandoned house. We were shaking the flashlights, trying to get them to turn back on, wondering what the hell could have killed them all at once—I think Tina had even put fresh batteries in hers before leaving her apartment. That is when I noticed a sort of glow coming from the second floor. By that time my eyes had adjusted a bit, and I was vaguely able to make out blobs and shapes in the dark, like the walls, a broken chair, and the stairs leading up to the floor above us, and it was there, on those stairs, that a hint of light was reflecting primitively for all to see. We shut up immediately. I took a step toward the staircase, but there was a hand on my arm. It was Henry—he whispered something like "Do not be stupid—where are you going?" but I kind of shuffled out of his grip and, with a deep breath, I placed one foot on the bottom step.

Before I took another step, the glow had gotten brighter. So I turned my eyes to the top of the stairs. That is when I saw the shape.

I assumed it was a man—it was definitely man looking. It was the craziest thing we had ever seen. Here was this silhouette of a giant man, backlit so you could not see his face, but apparently casting the very light it was silhouetted against. It was like a blue-white nightmare. I remember its hands clenching and unclenching. I remember it heaving like it was gasping for air. I remember the hands of my friends pulling on my clothing trying to get me to join their escape. I remember the sight of what looked like blood on the walls. The last thing I saw before I screamed was that thing, seemingly without moving a muscle, coming toward us.

We almost killed each other running out of Cold House. The front door, now a hindrance, was finally torn from its last hinge by running children. I was the last one out of the house. As I took the porch steps, my left leg plunged through old wood, tearing into my shin. I looked behind me, and that thing was framed in the doorway—menacing, unnatural. I could *feel* its light on my face, understand? I was utterly shell-shocked and I could not move. For some reason I knew it wanted me. This had been my plan, my idea, and this thing knew it. And it was going to punish me. I closed my eyes.

Then Henry was pulling me from the steps. He dragged me behind him, and I limped to keep up. We did not stop until we saw the lights of the streetlamps, shedding illumination and a bit of safety on our tiny bodies as we collapsed with the others next to the entrance to the woods. Nobody spoke. Someone was crying.

After a long time we all sort of stood as one and shambled quietly back toward the apartments. We were almost a walking funeral procession. As we came upon my building, Tina, Joe, and Brock silently peeled off to slip back into their own homes. Matt, Henry, and I crawled back into my room and, without another word, did our best to fall asleep. The next day we crawled out into the afternoon sunlight and sat against the wall of the complex, suddenly very vocal about what we had seen. Henry asked me if it had said anything to me, and I shook my head. Matt was convinced the thing had a hook for a hand, and nothing I said could change his mind. After a while Joe stopped over, and he was overly excited. He wanted to go back. I said I was in—so did Matt. Henry did not say anything. When we went to Tina's house, she said she was not feeling well and did not want to go. Brock's mother said he refused to even come to the door and asked us if we had been fighting. He never hung out with us again and avoided us around the complex.

As Matt, Joe, and I headed toward 14th, Henry suddenly had to go home. He said he would call me the next day after baseball practice. We were never very close after that day; I became more interested in music and comics, and he got more involved with sports. Tina still came around, but she flat-out refused to talk about Cold House. She even went as far as to say it never happened, that our imaginations had gotten the best of us.

The three of us who were left refused to pretend that it did *not* happen, and that afternoon we made our way back to the trails, leaping over the tripwires that now seemed pedestrian compared to what we had seen the night before. We came up on the house quickly and only really paused to take our time on the steps. As Matt and Joe bounded inside, I stopped for a second to look at the hole where my leg had broken through. I had cleaned up the gash without alerting my mother, who would have asked too many questions. I stood beside the hole, and immediately my mind went back to the moment when I was face to face with that supernatural spectacle, and I studied it a long time. So by the time I entered the house, the other two were already upstairs. I did not even notice that the front door was missing until I heard Matt and Joe shouting for me to "get up here NOW!" Moving to the bottom of the stairwell, I saw that there was nothing on the walls. No blood, but nothing that would have reminded me of blood in that ghostly light either. It was just gone.

As I came up the stairs—careful not to fall through anything again—I saw what they were going on and on about and could not believe it. The front door, which we had all smashed into in our haste to escape, eventually pulling it from the doorframe, was lying on the floor in an upstairs room. We recognized it from walking past it every day on our way to school. We recognized it from the split second we had seen it illuminated in the light of our torches before they had gone dead. It *was* the front door, and it was lying inexplicably in the middle of a room many feet away from where we had left it. However, we were not so interested in how it had gotten up the stairs into this room or who had put it up there in the first place. No, our attention was focused squarely on the word that was scrawled on its visage, almost scrubbed into the filth and grime that had built up on the door over the years:

"GO."

We ran like hell.

After school started that fall, I kept taking the trails through South Side Woods. Occasionally Matt and Joe did as well. Tina avoided it altogether. Brock in turn avoided *us* everywhere else. Henry waved at me at school, but by the time I moved away, we just were not best friends anymore, and that really kind of broke my heart. I left Iowa for Florida a few months later. I never saw any of them again, even after I moved back to Des Moines when I was sixteen. They had really just disappeared. Over the years I have forgotten their last names. If you asked me to imagine what they looked like as adults, I would not be able to pick them out of a random police lineup.

But I remember that night. I eventually told new friends about that night, and some of them made faces like I am sure you are making faces right now as you read about this. And yet most had had experiences as wild as mine. It was wonderful having friends who had gone through circumstances so close to my own, and we talked about what had happened and what we believed in. We believed in ghosts: real deal, holy-shit ghosts. We explored other abandoned houses together, never really finding anything as extreme as the incidents we had gone through before on our own. But our belief was strong—mine has never been stronger, for over the years I have seen things and heard things that are not only insane but also very real. I have a few pieces of proof that I have gathered, but much of what I have experienced is really just eyewitness accounts, and I will share them all right here. Before we go anywhere, though, before I start telling you these ghost stories, let me hit you with why I am writing this book in the first place.

You see, I am fairly famous—or infamous in most circles—for being, if you can excuse the term, a "devout atheist," which in a lot of ways can come off as a contradiction in terms. Cutting to the chase, *I do not believe in god*. Honestly, I really never have. I did not when I was too young to get out of going to church, and that continues right up until this moment, sitting in this chair, writing on this computer. I do not believe in God. I do not chastise or regard with disdain those who do, but my reaction to those who purportedly do terrible things disguised as "God's work" is acidic and maligned, to put it politely. I am just quick to judge those who are quick to judge, really.

So here is the question: How can I believe in ghosts . . . and not in God? How can I mock the very existence of Jehovah and his creepy winged minions while straight-facedly maintaining that there are ghosts, spirits, poltergeists, and haunts among us? How can I go on record with a whole book for that matter, dedicated to my version of the various events of my life, knowing full well that I might be regarded as a hypocrite at best, a nutcase at worst?

As you will find in this book, the running theory is a case of knowing versus believing.

I do not believe in God for various reasons. One, there is no real proof of the existence of God other than the usual suspects that the clergy and the like point to, such as man and the universe and all that jazz. But that, to me, is horseshit. Science has given us so many more bits of proof than God has, and even though He is lauded, He has no track record in my eyes. Just because the universe exists and man exists in it, that is no reason and no proof for the existence of an invisible man in the sky. I would sooner believe that Santa Claus was our creator, seeing as I get my wishes answered with the same relative consistency. God never saved me and Santa never gave me a harpoon gun, so fuck my life.

Two, too many of humanity's fingerprints are on God and his so-called achievements. Men wrote all of God's books, fought all of His wars, and have been the first to point out all of His miracles since he first blamed snow on His Holy Frosty Breath. Now why humans, who are vainglorious to a fucking fault, would give credit where it is not due is a psychotic fucking mystery to me, and yet people adhere to doctrine because they have been indoctrinated. It has been *hammered* into their skulls that God exists, even though men were so busy swinging the hammers at the time, they never realized they were using them on each other.

Three, God is about as real to me as those who reside in Asgard or in Valhalla. He might as well be in comic books, which is actually a good idea if you want the younger generation to take the idea of Him seriously. At the end of the day, God is infallible because man is fallible, and a lot of people need someone to believe in who is better than ourselves. Fair enough . . . but then why not believe in the Tooth Fairy? The Tooth Fairy at least pays you for pieces of your face that you were going to throw away anyway. God makes you put those same quarters in His collection plate, even though the church is tax exempt. Well, because of inflation, my son gets dollars for those molars, so a lot of tooth money goes to them now. Sounds pretty fucked up to me, but then again, none of it is mine.

I am appalled at the hate that His followers pour into the world like factories spewing pollution into country streams. I laugh at the self-proclaimed prophets who are too busy selling their own side of His story to consider that because their prophecies do not jibe with everyone else's accounts, there is no real continuity to His word. I abhor the fractious state of these worldwide Judeo-Christian and Islamic cults because they *all* think they are right. Religion has divided us more than it has brought us together, and normally anything that violent and dissenting would have been outlawed or driven from society if not for the fact that these pious pricks have their fingers in all the pies on Earth.

So yeah, I am not a God man, myself. But therein sits the fucked up rub: How can I be an atheist, a man who dismisses the grand conjectures of the righteous with no connection to religions and the like, and yet believe wholeheartedly in the existence of the paranormal? I do not pretend that one has anything to do with the other, but they have been intertwined since we were monkeys scrambling to make sense of anything that we could not eat, fuck, or excrete. Cynics will claim that my "eyewitness accounts" can easily be described as "flights of fancy," or "the trappings of an overactive imagination."

"There is no possible way that could have happened." "I do not believe you—you are a liar and a charlatan." (Well, no one ever called me a "charlatan," but, man, it would be great if they did). Oh, and the one that I hate even worse than those others: "You saw what you wanted to see and nothing more."

Let me fucking tell you something: I did not want to see this shit, and I still do not want to see this shit. These things have haunted me for a very long time, and anyone who has had to wrestle with terrible memories will know they *never go away*. I can see them as clearly now as I did when they happened. So you can be as skeptical as you like. I believe in ghosts because I have seen ghosts, and I do not believe in God because I simply have never seen God. There is a huge difference between the unexplained and the unsubstantiated. And yet all over this blue-green planet there are monuments, churches, statues, great paintings, books, and fanfare for He Who Sits in Heaven. People everywhere weep and cherish his name like a good piece of ass they had when they were busy wasting their twenties. But these same organizations have mocked people like myself, who have experienced firsthand the amazing sight of paranormal activity. Are they kidding?

With this book I am going to attempt to come to terms with this. I am going to tell you true stories that have happened to me—and there are several—and I am going to take you with me as I go searching for some proof, joining various "ghost-hunting" groups who do their best to gather information about and evidence of the existence of spirits. I will tell you other people's stories and get the other side of things—from nonbelievers in the unnatural and from the religious alike—so that I can make some sense out of all of this.

I am also going to do some things I have never attempted to do before, and if I fail miserably, I will certainly not attempt it again. I am going to try my hand at a version of "armchair science" and possibly formulate some sort of scientific reasoning for these mysterious things we call spooks. I have some pretty far-fetched tidbits percolating upstairs in the old Bank of Stuff and Nonsense, but the more I have gone seeking validation in certain arenas and schools of thought, the more I have found that some of these conjectures on my part are really not so out there as I had imagined, reinforcing my original hypothesis and bringing to an end my internal stalemate that would not allow me to say it out loud in the first place. So I am prepared to make a statement to the proper authorities on the matter and do my best to speak eloquently and persuasively about my bullet points and evidence. Unfortunately this does mean there will be a brief respite from my almost diabolic use of the word "fuck" for several pages. I know you are all expecting an unspecified amount, in addition to various demurrals about farts and dicks. But this *must* wait. I promise to circle back and regale you with these things at appropriate times, but it may mean that many pages will indeed be filled with ideas and forethought. You have my condolences, and I urge you to send angry letters to my editor—he loves those.

Fuck me, I am getting a bit bleak, right? This is *not* what you would expect from a Corey Taylor book. I know you have come to expect the odd pee pee story and ceiling fan scars. But I did not set out to write a sequel—I set out to write a continuation. People have the misconception that the first book was my life story. That is just completely false. This book and the previous tome are not autobiographies, and this is because I am not done *living* yet. Christ, I only turned thirty-nine while I was typing this tripe out—I am only halfway there! I do not even know what you would call these books technically, but they are not lifers just because I tell some assorted and sordid tales of woebegone days gone by. If they are anything, they are essays sprinkled with memoirs. But that looks a bit like crap on a plank of wood at your local W. H. Smith. So we will just shuffle this into the "nonfiction" section, although I am very confident various booksellers will shove these deep into the "music" section, much to my chagrin, of course. There is very little music discussed in these pages, so once again I am misunderstood. As the saying goes, however, shit happens. It seems like I always end up being the statue surrounded by rogue pigeons after a feast of berries and bugs. Bring it on, birds: if you strike me down, I shall become more powerful than you could possibly imagine . . . or so Lucas and Guinness would have you believe.

This book is more in line with *The Empire Strikes Back* than *The Wrath of Khan*. *Star Trek 2* was a proper sequel, while *Episode 5* was the next chapter in the story. Before you get all weird and bombard poor innocent folk who have no access to me and mine, there is a difference. So take it up with your solicitors. Better yet, I will see if I can build this specific debate into my Comic-Con panel entitled, "Shit or Split: A Pointless Argument Based Around an Innocuous Conundrum Only Three Hundred People in the World Will Lose Sleep Over." It will be a star-studded cast: the guy who played Biggs, the man who provides the arm for the puppet formerly known as Alf, one of the Jonas Brothers (they will appreciate the work), and Jonathan Frakes, if he is not too busy directing wonderfully bad movies on the Syfy Channel. I will be the asshole in the middle, because there is always an asshole in the middle. It is true: check your taint. What did Gandhi say? "Between the crack and the sack lies a friend you have to deal with your whole life." Wait—was that Gandhi or my Uncle Bill?

It looks like I went off on another tangent. I will never get that time back. Let's get back on track before I start talking about Benedict Cumberbatch. I agree: he *is* wonderful! Fuck—sorry . . . back to the book.

It has been a conundrum I have wrestled with for so long that it has actually made me question what I have seen, and yet with every replay in my mind, I know these things have happened. I *know* it. I know it as sure as I know that if I flip a switch, the lights will go on, or if there is gas in my car, it will start on the first turn of the key. Maybe that is not the same as believing—knowing always has a benefit of being there. Believing is more for the folks on the other side of the fence who are trying desperately to get me to come on over and join their holy hoedown. But in a way I believe as well. I believe when people tell me their stories. I believe when someone tells me that a place is haunted. I believe when I hear an EVP or see a video with something so bizarre that I have to watch it again to figure it out, then when I cannot figure it out, I stew over it for a very long time. I do all of this because I believe. But I have a *reason* to believe. I have been in those situations myself. I have no past experience with the Lord; I have no videos or sound bites to pull out to prove He is out there. And do *not* even get me started with the Muffin People, the ones who see His face in the side of a tortilla or a grilled cheese sandwich. What is it about the Almighty and grains, anyway? Apparently, Jehovah has a hard-on for complex carbohydrates.

So if you are like me—or even kind of like me—keep flipping the pages and we will see what we can see together. Sometimes there is an advantage to knowing the script before you have seen the movie. We all struggle with the known and unknown alike. It curbs our enthusiasm and keeps some of us moral. But it also keeps all of us looking, searching—hoping to see the other side of the metaphysical gymnasium, where all the kooks are bounding around, flinging giant red dodge balls at one another. You just know that at some point their attention is going to turn toward your side of things and all hell is going to break loose. By then you will not even know which direction the barrage is coming from, but you will know that *something* is coming. At least you will *know,* and that is all we really want. We just want to know. There are inconceivable mysteries beyond our horizons, out into the nether of space, millions upon millions upon millions of miles and lifetimes away that most of us neither have the capacity nor the patience to venture toward. Fuck, there are still places on this planet that man has not explored and there are species that we have not discovered, not to mention the rapid advances in technology on a regular basis. So for skeptics to tell me there is no way these things can exist or that what I am saying herein cannot be true is a pile of obstructive dick snot.

Let's face it: at the end of the day, aren't you glad there are still some fantastic things to figure out down here?

Leave math to the spacemen. Leave theory to the wish masters. Leave condemnation to hypocrites and bastards. Take one more deep breath, savor it, and plunge forward without thinking. Do not allow yourself hesitation. Do not allow yourself a moment of doubt. Follow your instincts and go where you never would have considered possible. The pale fabric of reality has so many hidden pockets that we can find some change in here somewhere—you just have to dig a little deeper to avoid the chewing gum and past mistakes. But if you give it time, we can find something wonderful, something to believe in. It is far better to explore and come back sated, albeit with more questions, than to stay behind and bitch because you are terrified of the answers that lie in the unknown. Sometimes the reward is richer when the journey was yours from the start. Sure, you enjoy the stories the truly brave bring back and share, but what really builds us all are the ones we share as one. Of course, that first step is the scariest. Do not worry—I am right here with you. No one here is going to scoff or judge or fuck with you. I will not allow it. That right there is the beautiful thing about new knowledge, really.

It may be strange, and it may scare the fucking shit out of you, but you will wonder.

YOU WILL WONDER.

BUT FIRST LET'S MEET OUR contestants

I HAVE THE SAME BIZARRE DREAM EVERY NIGHT. I am some sort of lone adventurer, standing at the edge of a mountain, gazing at a cave high up on a long precipice. I check my gear, which for some reason has a *lot* of weapons in it, including a harpoon gun (with necessary cable attached), rope, grappling hook, base-jumping parachute, and a backpack to keep it all in. I climb the side of the rock face, skillfully seeking purchase with knowledge I have never displayed before, until I finally reach the cave's mouth. Deftly, I pull a tiny flashlight from my utility belt and survey the deep blackness before proceeding forward.

I make my way through the caverns until I come upon what appears to be a massive subterranean hall, bigger than the main hall at Grand Central Station. I seem to be looking for something specific; there are several sets of train tracks and mining cars for transporting precious ores or coal in various areas of the underground hall. Just as I am wondering if it is still considered underground when you are high inside a mountain, the first screams shatter the silence like a glass chalice in the winter cold.

From every shadowy corner of the darkness, hundreds of beastly zombies spill into the light of my torch like a plague of locusts, cackling and spitting venom as they scatter and storm in my direction, sensing a threat and responding on instinct to the intruder's presence. But apparently I was prepared for this, because I immediately pull two Beretta 9 mills out of my side holsters and begin to fire with patience and accuracy. I empty the clips and eject them, swiftly sticking them into special holsters on my hips that will reload them as I pull two other guns (.357 Magnums) from shoulder slings to keep firing. When those are empty, I reach for the Berettas again. There are so many of these creatures that I know I cannot get them all. I am calm, though—

there is a plan. All I need to do is get to one of the mining cars. I know I can escape and get to where I need to go.

Firing for headshots, I race toward the tracks I need and jump in. The monsters try to grab at me, but I kick them away and get the car rolling down and away. The tracks lead across a giant chasm in the mountain, toward a tunnel that plunges into more darkness. But the place I am heading for is a small opening carved into the rock, far below. It looks like a door of some kind, and light billows from it like a shock of color on a dark night. So I grab my harpoon gun in one hand and the parachute in the other and propel myself into the air, tossing the silk back behind me while firing the harpoon gun, aiming at the wall closest to the door on the other side. The harpoon sticks into the granite, and I pull myself toward it with the rope attached, floating and moving as one, until I reach the doorway. Firelight illuminates my entry, and I step into the brightness and rub my eyes. I have made it; I fought my way through dangerous caverns and ungodly zombies to be here. I breathe a sigh of relief.

Then a voice yells, "Wipe your feet before you come in here!"

I know—it is a strange yet continuously awesome dream. It is filled with monsters, guns, caves, stunts, and a strange voice concerned with the cleanliness of a mountain hideaway. It has no basis in reality, it really tells no story, and to my knowledge has no real ending. Maybe I should sit and write it all down someday and see where it goes . . . oh shit, I think I just started to. You might be wondering why I have included this weird nocturnal adventure in this chapter. Well, let's see: no basis in reality, fantastic and unsupported claims, outlandish creatures, and an unseen person telling you what to do. Am I the only one thinking it feels a whole lot like religion?

If you have not noticed, I have never been a huge fan of organized religion and all of its minions. But it is not for a lot of the reasons you would think: the god thing, angels and shit, or Jesus and his magical fruit punch trick while walking across ponds. It is not that I am specifically against monotheism—I think the Greeks and Egyptians were fucking hilarious too. My main disagreement, apart from the mythology, is how divisive it makes every single person around the world. It seems like nothing makes a difference; if you do not have a problem with the other guy's god, you have a problem with his interpretation of god's word, even if it is the *exact same* god. We have been killing each other "in his name" ever since his was the only name left on the list—that is, depending on what language your list is in. It is utterly ridiculous. You think believing in ghosts is ludicrous? Try having a serious conversation about Noah and his weird cruise ship. The only distinctions between cults and religions are better PR strategies and about a million followers.

I will say that America has a better grasp on how organized faith can be manipulated and developed for better entertainment and distraction. Certainly, various countries and civilizations have spawned several important sects over the aeons of our existence. Northern Europeans have kept their Norse and Germanic paganism alive with the adoption of Asatru. China has given the world Taoism and Confucianism. India has produced Hindus, Buddhists, and Sikhs. Japan has Shinto, and the Middle East gave us Islam. Israel gave us Judaism *and* Christianity. But as far and varied as these theologies are, in my opinion, it seems America has the patent on taking basic ideas and making them weirder and more fucked up.

Mormons, Hare Krishna, Scientologists, Jehovah's Witnesses, Christian Scientists, Seventh-Day Adventists, Satanists (or Le-

Vayans)—from the Chopra Center to the Nation of Islam (an American invention), from Baptists to Wiccans, some Americans take faith and inject it with hell fire, bullshit, and good old-fashioned special effects. But one thing is for sure: for as many new doctrines as we churn out for the lunch rush, we still make sure not one of these gets along with another—or anybody else for that matter.

For a concept that is supposed to be inclusive, open, and understanding in its unconditional love, religion really does breed its share of maniacal, bigoted, prejudiced, and unscrupulous bastards, doesn't it? I know more atheists than zealots, and I can tell you the only things we argue about are which albums best sum up heavy metal. I mean, we as humans are always going to have a difference of opinion. My feeling is that religion only exacerbates our already individual positions.

Do not get me wrong—that is not to say there are not some atheists who are more thoroughly over the top than the righteous. Every sect has its balderdash, and nonbelievers can be just as unyielding as their spiritual doppelgängers. For atheists, *nothing* exists without true-blue proof, even if that includes life on other planets or our topic at hand: the existence of ghosts. But at least they can be reasonable from time to time if you can break it down on a one-on-one level. But the Right? The Flock? They are just not having it.

Then there are the little things that set me off about the whole pious situation, the undisclosed scar tissue that permeates the underbelly of my memories. In fact, let me tell you about the last time I went to Sunday-morning church. Mind you, the only reason I looked forward to mornings at Peace Lutheran was the promise of fried chicken that immediately followed Sunday service. When you are young, it is not really your choice, is it? But to be honest, there was a time when I looked forward to those Sundays because my grandmother took me, and she has always been my rock, my source of stability. So I joined her for prayer time (and the fried chicken).

But the older I got, the more I asked questions. I suppose this is what Catholics would refer to as "the crisis of faith." I mean, none of it made sense to me. Even as a child, the thought of an ancient, invisible stalker watching everything we do and keeping eternal records of such deeds was not only unbelievable but fucking terrifying to me. If you think about it, God does not watch over us; he fucking haunts us. In a way he is the original paranormal activity or, at the very weirdest, the OG John Hinckley.

Anyway, after a while I checked out spiritually and intellectually. I went to church to hang with my Grams and capitalize on the KFC clause. But I think she could tell I was not exactly emotionally invested in "the well-being of my immortal soul." She kept it to herself for the most part, even when I started sneaking in a Walkman to listen to my Metallica and Slayer albums. She had wanted me to go to Sunday school, which I did for a time, but no one in the classes wanted anything to do with me, including the assistant pastor who led the studies. Plus, I despised dressing up—still do to this day. Whenever I put on what is considered "formal attire," I always feel like I'm wearing someone else's clothes. There is nothing worse than walking around with the idea that you raided your Uncle Vernon's wardrobe. Oh, and why does God need you up and in the pews that damn early? During the school year I was basically wiping my ass with valuable weekend time. I do not know about you, but Saturday and Sunday are for doing fuck-all, not for freezing your ass off in a building with terrible circulation that smells like an opium den.

On my last day doing time in the holy holding pen I was sitting next to my Grams, waiting patiently for the end of the sermon. Distractedly, I pulled my headphones out of my jacket, and blocking its view from my grandmother, I snuck them to one side of my head so I could listen to Iron Maiden. I had just reached the end of side one (it was a cassette tape—tells you how long ago it was) when I looked up and realized the preacher had stopped talking. He and everyone around me were staring at me, including Grams, who had the look of breaking a few commandments in her eyes. I was kind of nervous. Why the hell were they looking at me? I was not doing shit! I was just biding my time until I could get out of those clothes and into a three-piece dinner with mash and gravy.

The congregation slowly went back to what they were doing. My grandmother, however, was not through with me, not by a long shot, as she was embarrassed by whatever I had done. She did not say a word; she just reached one hand over and slowly dug all four long fingernails into my forearm, immediately drawing my eyes to her and what she was about to say. My Grams is not a violent woman, but when she is in a foul mood, she can throw murder with her eyes. When she was sure she had my undivided attention, she leaned in close, paused, and whispered simply, "The next time you find it necessary to listen to your music here, maybe you should keep yourself from singing out loud." She held her nails there until she felt like she had made her point, then released.

Of course I felt terrible. The last thing I ever wanted to do in my life was disappoint my Grams. But I could not lie to myself anymore either: I was not, by any stretch of the imagination, cut out to be a holy-rolling churchgoer. We never discussed it, but the next Sunday when she went to Peace Lutheran, I remained in bed at home. With the exception of marriages and funerals, that was the last time I set foot in church of my own free will. My life as a fully formed heretic was underway. The one bummer was that if I still wanted fried chicken, I was going to have to get a job.

Let me tell you my biggest bitch about man and his God: when His name is invoked, it is almost guaranteed to create bullshit. Man and God start wars. Man and God fight advances in medicine, science, and other understandings of the universe. Man and God fight common sense with ignorance when it comes to politics, freedom, welfare, and safety. Man and God are doomed to explore the future with nothing more than dogmatic myths designed at a time when people still believed our health could be affected by curses and that leeches could drain the "bad blood" from our bodies, making us well. This is the so-called wisdom of the righteous. The problem is that religions are not updated; they are running on software that makes floppy discs look like time machines. The Christian bible, with all its flaws, is so out of sync with the modern world that if it were a different book entirely, people would scoff at any quoted passage or murmured anecdote. The same goes for any of the other tomes that lie at the center of the world's religions. The faithful languish in pure ridiculous stupidity, cribbing notes from their "textbooks" wherever it suits them, regardless of context or relevance.

Look, I know why religions were created—or at least I can make a fairly educated guess why people would reach for truth in fantasies. For all intents and purposes, I like the fact that gods were invented to explain things we did not understand, like the stars, volcanoes, and the weather. After we were savvy enough to start putting the pieces together ourselves, I know why the purpose of the gods changed to reflect how we treat each other: some of us needed guidance, or at least some sort of consequences for our actions. We as people were still too unrefined to understand how to exist together peaceably. We thrived when the rules were laid out, so I get that.

Ladies and gentlemen, allow me to personally cash your reality check.

It is now 2013. I am here to tell you that if you still need a guidebook that was written when people were still trying to marry camels, you have bigger issues than how to live your life. The human race has been gifted over the centuries with fantastic minds: philosophers of such extraordinary knack that we have thrived in leaps and bounds with each generation. This same gene pool has given us scientists and mathematicians of the highest caliber who have unlocked the secrets of space, time, and our own genetic codes. With every step toward spiritual freedom, I am proud to say we get a little farther away from the shackles of superstition. But it is almost always the elders of our race who cling to this horseshit like flies at an outhouse, and those same people are almost always in positions of power, using the "good word" to control the minds—and the votes—of the flock.

But here is the anomaly: in a lot of ways the church—especially the Catholic Church—encourages our scientific discoveries, and always has. It invites breakthroughs of profundity because it is convinced they are evidence of the existence of God. It waits for breakthroughs from the various particle colliders around the world because that, to them, is another example of "intelligent design." Aside from trying to give His Bigness credit for these things, I have to have respect for that. But that respect stops dead when you take into consideration the evidence of molestation attached to that religion. In my opinion, suppression of the sexual drive inspires dark repercussions, manifesting in the worst possible way: destruction of our children's innocence. If the Catholic Church actually *did* something about it, I might cut it some slack. But it seems to me that some of the various papists in charge have decided to engage in a predatory witness relocation program, shuffling offenders around to different cities—in some instances different states and countries—and pretending that will quell the darkness in these monsters. All this does is maintain the evil status quo. If this is the case, these people should be fucking castrated and chucked into shark-infested waters.

Let's get back on topic. Religion, when it is organized and focused, crumbles foundations and judges the good and bad alike; there are no exceptions when the righteous get their blood up. Hell, America was founded on the very principle that church and state should always be separate . . . well, technically anyway. The original settlers of the colonies that would eventually become America purportedly came to the New World to escape persecution for their religious beliefs. I say fair enough on that—no one should be demonized or tortured for what they believe or how they live their life. But many of these spiritual refugees also came to this land to baptize the heathens who already lived here. To the tribes who already had houses in North America, there was no such thing as the "New World"—there was just home. Unfortunately, the new tenants were told in the Bible that there would be no second coming of Christ until the *entire* world was evangelized. So the settlers came here, ready to "save" the indigenous populace. They soon found themselves freezing and starving, so they eventually started slaughtering the very people they were trying to baptize so they could raid their food storages. So in a way the doorway to the resurrection of Jesus is America's front porch, and it is stained with the blood of innocent peoples just living their own way of life, with no real need for European zealots to save them.

My slaveholding forefathers knew that we would accomplish nothing if the slavish rhetoric of the Church bound our hands. Now look at us: America is one of the most pious, one of the most self-righteous and judgmental countries on the planet— shit, in the Milky Way galaxy. America is also ranked twenty-fifth globally when it comes to education, and we have not produced a true genius-level visionary in forty years. Okay, fine, Steve Jobs and Bill Gates, but all they did was saddle us with bigger and better distractions, thus cementing our spot at twenty-five. The American sects are insane, crying wolf whenever their ignorant blood starts boiling and protesting when we try to do something crazy . . . like educate people on gun control or design stronger, more hardy foods that can be grown in the more inhospitable parts of the world. They hate gay people and discourage their rights to get married, even though gay couples are statistically more stable than hetero couples, especially when those numbers are padded by professional welfare cases and teen pregnancy, which might not happen as often if the Religious Right did not fight sex education at every turn. They are so misinformed and opinionated that listening to them "speak intelligently" is a painful and incredible contradiction in terms. It is like reading from the worst script imaginable . . . or the best script of all time, depending how you like your movies.

Then again, I am sure some people will feel the same way when they listen to me go on and on about paranormal activity. But here is the difference: I am not saying you have to believe in what I believe. Modern religions damn you if you do not while also damning you if you do, depending on your taste for deities.

I guess that would be where my all-purpose "Go Fuck Yourself" gesture comes in handy. It is pretty simple: give the middle finger, making sure to flick your wrist upward as you do, and blow your raspberries (for the uninitiated, that means stick your tongue out and "SHPPPPPPPPP"). I know I have intimated that the God folk may be more prone to jumping on my spooky bandwagon than most others, but at the same time there is a fanatical, conspiracy-theorist glint in the eyes of the righteous that I can do without. In dodge ball you do not pick the weakest links; you pick the ones who can handle the job load.

Just between you and yours, I know and believe the difference comes down to knowing and believing, if you can allow the words to play. I know the things I have seen are real. I recall the events with a historian's clarity. I can close my eyes and remember the room I was in, the clothes I was wearing (or had just taken off), the look on my face, and the cool tingle that ran up my spine. Fear can be a strong bookmark when it comes to recall. But that is just it: knowing and believing are so different that they might as well be magnetic opposites. A person who knows can draw on the experience to use the framework of explanation in sculpting a stronger foundation of acceptance; a person who just believes may eventually find him or herself living in a house that never existed or stuck in a position of seeing their cellophane walls dissolve under the warm rain of truth and fact.

Religious zealots believe what they do with no proof or understanding. Worse yet, they treat others by the Book, a tome that is older than most accepted behavior in this day and age. I am not just jumping on the Christians, although my experiences have dealt mostly with their ilk. It could be said that some devout Muslims treat women like second-class citizens at best and used tissue at worst. In fact, most religions have almost all been severely matricidal, spiritually speaking. Women are denigrated and limited to backup rolls so the "men" in charge can carry all the glory and take all the credit. In the world's most sectionalized cultures women are punished and often murdered for doing something as unthinkable as voicing their opinion. If this is what religion can accomplish, then I would rather throw my own little faithless tea party, thank you very much.

Once again, this book is meant to start a conversation. My last book dealt with sin; this one, among other things, deals with death and what might come next. I had a talk once with a very good friend who is an odd mix of comic-book geek and devoted Catholic. We were having some afternoon java and comparing notes on things like the paranormal. He tried to explain to me that, although he truly believed in ghosts and had seen his share of strange occurrences, he was convinced that most spirits were people who had sinned in life, had paid no religious attrition, and were doomed to walk the Earth until their sins were forgiven. I frowned a bit because that raised several questions, but I started with a few precursors first: "So you are saying Earth is a sort of prison for the unrepentant?"

"Correct," my friend, who we will call Carl, answered.

"Well, being Catholic, doesn't that rub with the whole 'Purgatory' setup?"

He paused for a minute, then said, "Not really, when you consider that perhaps the glimpses we get of these spirits are simply Purgatory's thin spots. And Purgatory is essentially temporary Hell—those souls will eventually go to Heaven. The spirits on Earth might just be the ones who cannot recognize they are dead. Once they do, they will go to Hell." He smiled and drank his coffee.

I just stared at him.

He blinked and said, "What?"

It took me a second to finally blurt out, "That cannot be what you believe. Are you *shitting* me?"

"What is wrong with that explanation?"

"Where the fuck do I start? What about the ghosts of children? What about the souls of the truly decent? How can they all be sinners, just waiting to get clued in to the fact that they are dead so they can go to Hell?"

"Why does that bother you?"

"When do you suppose a six-year-old found the time to do something worthy of being damned for eternity?"

Carl then did something I had never seen him do before: he took on the air of someone who had a certain knowledge and truly felt sorry for the ignorant, giving me a knowing smile that almost made me punch the shit out of him. "People commit sin, no matter what the age."

You have got to be . . . "You know damn well I do not believe in Hell."

"C. T., just because you do not believe, that does not mean it is not true."

"Oh, and where do you suppose Hell lies—just below the topsoil or just above the Earth's magma?"

"That is not funny."

"It was not a joke! And let's not forget the fact that you contradicted yourself. How can these supposed 'oblivious dead' be forgiven their sins but *still* go to Hell? Is that not part of the whole Heaven gift basket?"

Carl left.

Subsequently, we did not talk for a while.

Thankfully I have other friends who have no legs in Christ's shackles. But the funny thing is that I do not mind many of the things that Jesus supposedly preached (oh yeah, I am also one of those weirdoes who is not completely convinced that Jesus ever really existed). I like the idea of turn the other cheek. I adore that the meek shall inherit the earth. I enjoy the miracle section—the loaves and the fishes, the water into wine. The water-into-wine story gives me enough pause, however, to draw some connections here and there. I call it the "Miracle Hypothesis": there is the walk-on-water story and then there is the water into wine story. There is a tidy little parallel, because when you think about it, people in the old days—even to this day—use their feet to stomp grapes to make wine, right? Well, we all know that no one can actually walk on water unless there is a very long dock submerged just under the surface in the shallow end. Sooooo . . . maybe Jesus was making wine at a party for some people who had never seen how wine was made before. Different people told the story enough that it really became two different stories: walking on water (or grape juice really—it would have never had time to ferment) and turning water into wine (because these confused ignorant people might have assumed the liquid was water before the truth came out). Is it a stretch? Of course it is a stretch, most assuredly so. But that is what religion and the Bible are all about—stretching stories into scripture and, hundreds of years later in America, the Official Land of the Gullible, turning scripture into "fact." Just to recap: it is possible that a person named Jesus stomped fruit for wine, people saw this being done, and through an ancient version of the game Telephone, a tale of one man making beverages for a soiree becomes two miracles that have the feel that they were mutually exclusive.

Before you ask: yes, this is what I do with my time when there is nothing on TV and I have had too much coffee. I debunk outlandishly dumb religious tales in an even more outlandish way. To quote the Christian Sasquatch: judge not lest ye be judged yourself.

Between the Council of Nicea and the nineteenth-century advent of Dispensationism, it really is a wonder that more Christians do not sit up, put their newspaper and coffee down, and say, "Wait a minute . . . *what the fuck*?" It all appears to be based on faulty math. Where does this leave us then? I will tell you: it leaves us in a climate in which everyone has a different interpretation of *that book*, and it is not specifically relegated to Christianity. Muslims fight Christians openly because they are convinced Christians are wanton agents of the Antichrist. Both team up on the Jewish culture for no real reason other than they feel better when they both have a common enemy. I have not seen a collaboration this juvenile since the fourth graders teamed up with the third graders to beat the fifth graders at kickball.

Maybe it is because religion is not sexy enough for me—or for other atheists while we are on the subject. Mind you, it is not like ghost stories get teenagers running for the bathrooms, embarrassed by the sudden tightness of their pants. But the God Chronicles have never inspired heavy petting either. That could be the issue, and I believe I have a solution for that. It is an idea I had years ago while writing my columns for *Rock Sound* in the UK. You see, even though I am not a fan of the cloth, I am a fan of certain bits of its mystery, like the whole God vs. Satan storyline. I really dig "good versus evil" because I like it when things feel right while other things are clearly wrong. In my first book I pointed out that it is only when the waters get muddied with the gray areas that we have problems as knuckle-dragging human meat. However, it is a bit tired. We get it—the theological throw-down will tear us to shreds with all the might of a million Hiro-shimas and whatnot. So it is a foregone conclusion. But when we think of these opposing deities, they are always male. You think of Morgan Freeman from *Bruce Almighty* as God and Robert De Niro from *Angel Heart* as the Devil, and you send them spinning toward each other for cosmic battle. My suggestion is: What if they were female?

Imagine Elizabeth Hurley from *Bedazzled* as the Devil—mmmmmmm! Then conjure up Alanis Morrisette as God from *Dogma*—ooh! Now, drape them each in their own leather bikinis: Hurley in flat black and Morrisette in shiny white. *Now, we are fucking getting somewhere!* Okay, now that we have our outfits, where and what would the battleground be? I would like to as-sume that we would all agree some place tropical—the Caribbean, for example. That just leaves us trying to sort out what the arena would comprise. Some would immediately run for mud wrestling, but I disagree. Mud tends to obscure the, ahem, obvi-ously interesting mishaps that come with moist wrestling. Inter-estingly, I have several other alternative solutions (yes, the pun *is incredibly* intended). What if our lovely Lord-like ladies tore at each other in honey? I know, right? I like that because it brings to mind Ann Margaret in *Tommy*. The viscosity is great, and it is not too opaque that we cannot readily see where the heat is com-ing from. Another delicious idea is Jell-O! Ah, I recall the grand days when gelatin wrestling was a risqué melodrama, and I do so with a faint and knowing smile in my heart. Pudding would fol-low that train of thought, but we run into the same problems we had with mud (just not as edible, admittedly). Alas, I feel I must bring this conundrum to a screeching halt with the obvious an-swer, an answer that will give our competitors the desired (snicker) and wonderful immersion that an epic conflagration such as this truly deserves. Friends and enemies, the only real answer is *oil*. Yes, corn or veggie, motor or olive, I do not know about you, but *my* God and Devil will fight for the lives of saints and sinners clad only in biker bikinis, completely saturated in warm oil. It may not be where the Bible was heading with the Armageddon thing, but as Mary Poppins belted out as she brainwashed the children: "A spoonful of sugar makes the medicine go down." If that is where religion is heading—two beautiful mythical forces going at it dressed in cow hide, drenched in melted oleo—I just might sign up for the Jesus bed and breakfast myself.

Then again, to quote George Clooney, "I may be a bastard, but I'm not a fucking bastard."

Whenever something unbelievable happens, I always hear some fucking sportscaster or news anchor (read: talking head) say, "the world's best fiction writers could not have come up with something as outlandish as this!" Um, I hope no one minds, but I strenuously object to that. You see, a good fiction writer *could* come up with stuff like that, whatever "that" actually happens to be. It does not take much in this day and age to create something completely and unabashedly false and fantastic. It is real life that is constantly throwing us for a loop, with chaos and entropy and all the crap that comes with it. Real life cannot be controlled—it can only be lived and adapted to, equally. It is when people start meddling and proceed to build myths out of molehills that shit gets complicated. You see, people wrote the Bible. People created God. The problem erupts when you try to sell it the other way around. So "the world's best fiction writers" could come up with a concept like God and all the trimmings, and we suffer aeons later when the fiction is treated as fact and we allow the witless to determine what we should do to evolve.

There it is: control. The faithful cannot handle when others try to do something without invoking God's name, so they try to control the outcome or its completion. It is my belief that man (or woman—I want to be inclusive) will go nowhere as long as the Holy Monkey is on our back. We will never make it to the next level of existence with flawed thinking. There is a reason that anyone with any reason resists the so-called intelligent design theory, and that is because it is *not* a theory. The faithful say that in order to be fair, this theory should be taught in school right alongside the theory of evolution. Well, you holy yocals, here is the rub: the theory of evolution is a scientific theory because it is verifiable. That is the whole reason it is a *scientific* theory. Intelligent design is *not* science—it is mythology that is not based on factual data that can be observed and tested. You are so busy trying to be right and so set in your ways that you never bothered to learn the actual definition of the term "scientific theory," and I am so disgusted with your ignorant behavior that I will not provide it for you herein. Let me just say that the definition does *not* involve the words hope, guess, myth, unverifiable, or bullshit. So keep your hopeless guess-ridden unscientific myth out of my school system, and I will do my best not to throw shit at you just after your gorgeous buffets on Easter Sunday.

My friends, I do not want to be an asshole. I do not want to sound like a dick-faced hypocrite. But I am also not going to sugarcoat a bunch of fucked up delusions just so they taste better when I try to swallow them. If faith works for you, please understand that I will not judge you for that—in fact, I envy you. I wish I could suspend my reality that far over the precipice, like that dream I have in the mountain that I will never comprehend. But I am saddled with that prick of a burden named cynicism. Does that make me a hypocrite when it comes to my adherence to the paranormal? Maybe—actually, more like yes, absolutely. And yet who knows? Like I said, I know what I saw and experienced. We will get to all of that—and I do mean *all of it*—soon enough.

Sometimes I wonder why I am trying so hard to get to that cave in the mountain. I wonder about who that voice belongs to, the voice that is so concerned about me wiping my feet in a dirty-ass cave. I wonder why those zombies were protecting him or even *if* they were protecting him. What lies beyond that doorway? What is that man's name? Who would have ever thought I would have the balls to *base*-jump? Sure, I am in a mountain, but that does not mean it is not equally terrifying. But where does this fantasy come from, anyway? Maybe I will never know, and quite frankly I am alright with that.

In the end we all need that rope to keep us tethered to our lives, leading us through our own strange caverns and pitfalls until we eventually find that faceless man in the mountain to give us the clues we think we deserve. Maybe my dream is some kind of accepted version of St. Peter, guarding the pearly gates with his ledger and his questions. That could mean there is a bit of my sodden brain that desperately wants to have that kind of faith. I do not know why—maybe to belong, maybe to have some semblance of order and dictation. Maybe I am just getting to that age when it feels easier to stop fighting the waves and let the current sweep me out into the deeper pieces, so to speak. But my fucking mind will never relent to that: I know me way too well. I have been finding ways to break rules and bend popular thought my whole life, armed only with uncommonly common sense. Hell, I even have a hard time giving a red shit about wearing underwear with jeans, for fuck's sake. You think I could ever give in and buy the thought of a spiritual overseer up in the cumulus keeping score on all the monkeys on his blue-green marble? Not only keeping score, but ready at any minute to file us in the "ETERNAL BURN" folder for something as irrelevant as eating the wrong meat on the wrong day while also working on another verboten day? Maybe I myself could not make this up, but somebody else did. I know this in my shitty little heart, and I will never submit.

Ever.

I am no Einstein. Hell, I am no *actual* Albert Einstein. But I do know this: "The word God is for me nothing more than the expression and product of human weakness, the Bible a collection of honorable, but still purely primitive, legends which are nevertheless pretty childish." That, my friends, is a quote from the actual Albert Einstein. What I have tried to say in a chapter he says with one complex sentence. If I could be allowed to act as a posthumous Einstein hype man for a brief but glorious second or two, I rest my fucking case. We will have a little more from our friend with the crazy hair later on in the book, but for now I am content in my happiness that, at least on paper (more pun intended), he and I appear to be on the same page (that was the end of said pun).

Oh, by the way—my computer just suggested that Einstein's quote was grammatically unsound. Cheeky fucker.

Lately people have been asking me a lot of questions about death, most likely because I have lost a lot of people extremely close to me in the last four years. However, they never ask me if we come back as a spirit. It always comes down to heaven and the dead stampede into the great corral. I keep my answers succinct and solid: I have no idea what happens when you die. I could not care less, really. You say maybe this is just because of all the misery and shit I went through when I was younger, but my attention is squarely on the present, on life, and less on death and whatnot. Maybe when I get older I will cast a better eye toward that end of the gym. But right now I do not and will not give an opinion on the more cloudy section of the heavens. I will say, however, that I believe there is a better shot of walking the Earth after you are gone than ascending toward some unseen dimension between one of the spheres in the wide sky.

There will be a day when I die, and the only thing I want is to be cremated. I want some of my ashes made into Life Gems for my wife and family. Some more of the ashes I want sprinkled into various ashtrays outside of grocery stores in Des Moines, in salute to the days when I was homeless—people always light a smoke when they get out of their car, take two drags, and put it out in those ashtrays. When you are broke and homeless, those are the best places to get free cigarettes. Depending on what my wife wants, the rest of my ashes can be buried next to her or commingled with her own ashes. Thus ends what I think about for after I die. Let's put it this way: if I wake up in Heaven, I will shit myself. Then I will quietly head for the exit—I know when and where I am not wanted.

Well, that is my side of it. That also means we are ready to get to the good shit. Both teams are aware of the rules. They have told us a little bit about each other, likes and dislikes, and what life is like back in Bucktooth, Wisconsin. They know what is at stake, and they know we are playing for keeps. So no waiting for a commercial break, and no flipping a coin to see who goes first—square your stance, bear down on it, pray you do not hit any whammies, and prepare yourself.

Time to play the Feud.

THE MANSION

IF YOU EVER FIND YOURSELF in Hollywood looking for something to do that does not have the unholy stench of "tourist" all over it, here is something you can do that will not cost you a dime. Find Sunset Boulevard and turn up Laurel Canyon, heading toward the valley. You will pass Mt. Olympus (sort of—it is not the "real" one). You will pass the neighborhoods where all the rock stars in the sixties and seventies lived, from the Mamas and the Papas and the Eagles to Jim Morrison and Frank Zappa. You will also pass the little general store on the corner where the groupies waited for all these said rock stars to come and shop or maybe just take one of them home. Once the corner store is in your rearview mirror, all that is left is a stoplight and two turns. You will pass Lookout Mountain, and then the road straightens out for a split second. Quick—turn your head to the left. Did you see the sprawling mansion set hard against a slope in the Hollywood Hills?

You just saw a haunted house.

The house at 2451 Laurel Canyon has a very strange history, and depending on who is telling it, you might get a different history each time. Owned by Rick Rubin, it has been called "The Mansion," or "The Houdini Mansion," and "The House Bess Houdini Built after Harry Died." After all the research I have done and all the available info I have combed through, the only name that fits is the first. The fact is that Harry Houdini never lived at 2451, nor did his wife build it after he died. To be honest, no two people can agree on when it was actually built. Some say it was erected in 1918, one year before Harry Houdini relocated to Hollywood to get into "moving pictures." Other people maintain that the estate was built in 1925 by Richard Burkell. Harry's proper "house" was at 2400 Laurel Canyon, but even that is open to debate. There is no documentation to show that Houdini even owned a home in Los Angeles; he and his wife reportedly used the guesthouse of department store magnate Ralf Walker, and Bess Houdini continued to stay in that same guesthouse until Walker's death. This is basically how 2451 Laurel Canyon got the name Houdini House. But legend has it that there was so much more. According to myth and nonsense, there was a sprawling castle with parapets and hidden tunnels, passageways for the great escapist to visit his mistress with his wife being none the wiser. You would think she might have noticed all the construction, but I do not judge; I do not even check expiration dates. I just sniff and hope.

Popular usage by a user-friendly populace has perpetuated the assumption that the Mansion at 2451 had anything to do with Houdini and vice versa. I can relate—hey, it is a wonderful story to swap over margaritas at an afternoon get-together. Gossip and rumor are a lot like trading cards—the more rare and outlandish they seem to be, the more valuable they are to all involved. So everyone from housewives to hippies gave this crispy quip a longer shelf life than it might have expected. I am confident Rubin let that bet ride as well. Nothing makes the heart grow fonder than the proposition of mystique . . . and a sweet pool.

The confusion does not stop there. Some people claim Errol Flynn lived in the Mansion in the thirties, but others claim his only real home in the area was at Mulholland Farm. Then again, if you read the book *Errol Flynn Slept Here*, he crashed at a lot of places over the years. So maybe that one has a glimmer of merit. I do not think he lived there per se, but he might have gotten his swashbuckling groove on. I think I read somewhere that he liked to make fuck with his socks on—either he had bad circulation or he just had a penchant for sexing in snowdrifts.

Sorry—that had dick and balls to do with here, there or anywhere . . .

What is true finally is that the Mansion burned down with everything else in the area in 1959, when fire ravaged the hills. From what I have been able to research, a woman named Fania Pearson eventually purchased the properties on all four corners of Laurel Canyon and Lookout Mountain and owned them from the sixties to the mid-nineties. These included the "real" Houdini House, the Tom Mix/Frank Zappa Cabin, and the Mansion. To this day there are people who live in the canyon who doubt Houdini ever even visited there. But by then the legend had taken on a life and purpose of its own. Never mind all the evidence and documentation—that does not stop people from seeing his "ghost" walking the grounds and frightening children. Nor does it keep groups from trying to hold séances somewhere on the property to contact the Great Houdini. The Master of Magic is making the rounds more frequently in death than in life.

The residents in the canyon have legends that have nothing to do with Houdini and his immortal coil, like how the Mansion was a squat in the heady decades of rock, roll, and the Sunset Strip. There was even a rumor that Vasquez's gold (huh?) was supposedly hidden beneath some of the foliage on the trails that run up the back of the house. One tale features a mentally deranged gentleman who was convinced he was Robin Hood reborn, and the canyon was Sherwood Forest; children going to and from Wonderland Elementary had to beware of "arrows" and old English. Most believe this is who people truly saw when they claimed it was Houdini back from beyond the grave. I may not be a rocket scientist, but I think I can spot the difference between a spirit and a crazy fucker.

You might be asking yourself if I am defeating the purpose of this book by debunking this house and its charm. What am I doing answering questions that no one wants to ask? I am merely setting the tone for my experiences by setting the record straight on the whole Houdini thing; none of my stories have anything to do with the King of Cuffs and Cards. From what I can tell, there is no need for his presence. Tales run rampant of inhabitants being murdered or committing suicide in the Mansion. People allegedly overdosed or were assaulted at punk parties during the seventies and eighties. One story has the son of a well-to-do furniture maker pushing a scorned lover to her death from one of the balconies. Another involves finding the body of a man dressed in a tuxedo hanging from the ceiling in one of the bedrooms when the place was vacant; this was apparently in response to a rebuked proposal. I do not know what would possess a man dressed as Archibald Leach to kill himself in a vacant property, but if Homo sapiens have a defining characteristic, it is the one in which they reach for the highest and brightest example of bat-shit crazy.

Remember the one about Tuxedo Man—it will have more meaning later.

My time in the Mansion begins in 2003 when I moved in with the rest of Slipknot to begin the recording of what would be *Vol. 3: The Subliminal Verses.* The funny thing is that I did not even stay there that first night; I went out on the town and passed out at a stranger's house. That was par for the course during the first month of making that album—crashing at someone else's house. I would walk up the driveway each morning, hung over and miserable, but I would always wave and say hello to the groundskeeper, who would smile and shake his head at my appearance from the street.

Yes, I got up to some smarmy shit in that era. I did indeed have several cab company phone numbers programmed in my phone just in case one of my friends refused to take me out drinking. I did engage in some crazy belligerent escapades with certain people who lived or squatted in Los Angeles and its surrounding boroughs, suburbs, and hamlets. I did make a fool of myself at parties and the Rainbow Bar and Grill on a regular basis. I did have a drunken conversation with Ron Jeremy at a porn star's birthday party for twenty minutes before I realized he was getting a blowjob the whole time. But that is not the type of book I want to write for you today. I mention these things in passing right now so I can satisfy your tiny craving for the outlandishly scintillating; now we can get back to the task at hand, and I can tell you about my other experiences in that swarthy expanse. So there was your cookie. Good to go? Moving on.

My paranormal experience with the Mansion started the way most crazy things do: with a dare.

Some of the guys and I were exploring—getting the lay of the land and checking out the place. We were running up and down the trails in the back and scampering across the bridge on the side of the house. We ran up and down and back up the stairs, looking on every floor and leaning into every room. No one had chosen their respective bedrooms yet because the majority of the band had not arrived. So we had the run of this decadent fucking keep—the house is the size of a museum. If I can be allowed to gush a bit, the place is fantastic. I was in love with it from day one. We were acting like kids, and I was having a ball until we made our way into the basement.

I know there are not many basements in California, but I believe this one was at one time a wine cellar. There was a bedroom (of sorts—it had a bed and a lamp against a brick wall), and there was also an odd room just to the left with a strange door that slid to the side. I opened it and darkness answered. There was just absolutely no light inside—no bulb or window or anything. And even though the house's air conditioning had not been turned on yet and we were all sweating to death, this room was ice cold. Someone blurted out, "Get in there—I dare you!" So I did. I walked to the middle of the room and smiled as they closed the door. This is nothing, I thought to myself.

Then something walked right through me.

Seeing as I was in complete ebon blackness, I felt it but did not see it happen. This, however, made it infinitely worse. One minute nothing was happening, the next I was pushed backward with the violation. The only way I can describe this sensation is that it was like being possessed by the winds of Antarctica. No, that really does not cut it either. It was like someone made of ice tried to hold me. I cried out a little in the dark, and from behind the door I heard the guys laugh. I scrambled for the door handle, threw it open, and fled upstairs. Everybody was taken aback. "What happened?" they asked. I would not answer. I just walked around for a while, trying to beat some warmth into my limbs and not really accomplishing anything.

Unfortunately for the boys and me, this was only the beginning.

Gear and amps alike malfunctioned. A whole session was lost because a strange loop started playing in the headphones that would only go away when we finally shut down the whole goddamn mixing board and recording unit. Things would disappear and reappear in other rooms, rooms that were clear on the other side of the house. Everyone would tell me their stories, but only when no one else was around. They had no idea it was happening to everybody. People staying in the renovated garage under the house would wake up to someone screaming in their face, but no one would be there. Invisible visitors would sit on their beds. The dogs in the house were going ape shit; I could hear them late at night losing their minds, then find out the next day after investigation that there was not a single person around, not even a California varmint.

I have had so many people caution me against writing this book because of the incredible amount of cynicism that will wash my way like garbage on the waves—just surfing the shit to gain access to my little world in order to bring me down. My response has always been the same: it is not my fault that there are millions of human beings who refuse to believe in something fantastic. Of course, by saying that, I allow myself to fall under the same scrutiny I myself have reserved for people who believe in gods. I offer you this simple solution: read this book for entertainment, amusement, or peace of mind. I do not really care— no skin off my dick.

About a month or so into my tenure at the Mansion, my first real "holy fuck" moment happened. But before I regale you with this, I have to give you some geographical background. In layman's terms, you have to know the lay of the land. Let me set the scenery . . .

There are several rooms and wings in the Mansion. There is a wing like a tree house that has a set of stairs and a bedroom that you can enter using a bridge. There are also three rooms at the top of the main staircase, a hallway to the left of the stairs that leads to two other bedrooms, and yet another staircase, which takes you to two more bedrooms and the "pool house." There are also bedrooms in the aforementioned basement and "finished" garage. The place is a massive lesson in futility, honestly; paths that take you to several different places, none of which are the exact location that you were looking for in the first place. One time when I was there alone, I got so fucking lost that I finally gave up, went outside, and walked all the way around the house just so I could go in the front door and get my bearings straight. It is a beautiful yet confounding construction.

Anyway, Clown and I shared the two rooms at the end of the hallway leading away from the stairs—last door on the left and straight on til morning. It was essentially one room split into two sections; Clown had the half with the balcony and the sunshine, and I had the half with the bathroom and the thermostat. It worked out great for everyone. I later learned it was the same room that Cameron from American Head Charge stayed in when that band was recording there. The story goes that he lasted one night; something happened after that first night that drove him into the control room to sleep, and that's where he stayed—for the entire recording process. Someone told me that he never went back in that room. Well, Clown and I were never anything if not completely and utterly obstinate. But in retrospect I can see why Cameron bailed.

On the evening in question Clown was not even there—he had gone back to Iowa to see his family. So I had the place to myself, and as people alone are prone to do, I was acting like the parents were away for the week. I was using the bathroom with the door wide open and running around buck-ass nude. My clothes and stuff were strewn throughout my hovel with not a care as to who would trip on them or what it was they were stepping on. That night it was "Enter at Your Own Risk." Now I should explain something: there was only one door into our bedrooms. There were balcony doors, sure, but there was no way for anyone to enter using those; we were on the second floor, not to mention the fact that they were locked when Clown was away.

He always locked those doors when he was gone, and I respected that—I never went in his room anyway. So there was only one door in and out of our wing, and that door opened into the hall-way. The door was also perpendicular to the bathroom door, cre-ating a sort of "L" shape in the front corner of our entryway. Basically, whoever came in, our bathroom was the first thing you saw, on the left. Get it? Got it? Good.

So I was alone in our rooms. The door to our room was shut and locked. The doors to the balcony were shut and locked. But the door to the bathroom was wide open. I was taking a shower, getting ready to hit the town with a vengeance. This was back in my Long Hair Days, so I had just washed a quart of shampoo out of my hair whilst simultaneously preparing to throw a liter of conditioner back in just to be able to get a brush through it. I was in a great mood—singing along to the Bee Gees (what? It was "You Should Be Dancing"!) and washing all my filthy bits that needed immediate attention. The shower curtain was open a smidge, and I could see the room from my vantage point. I looked up.

A man in a tuxedo walked past the open door, staring right at me.

I froze for a half-second . . . then vaulted out of the shower, racing into the bedroom naked, with way too much conditioner on my head. It was literally no longer than a second. But there was nobody there. I was alone in the room. All the skin on the back of my neck turned into white hackles. I searched the room for unlocked doors or windows, but the place was tight as a drum. The more I thought about it, the more I realized that from that angle, Tuxedo Man would have had to walk *through the door* of our bedroom—not open it and come in, but through it. After about a minute it suddenly dawned on me that I was soaking wet and without apparel, freezing my ass off. So I calmly yet cautiously made my way back into the bathroom to finish my shower. But my joyous mood had fled. I finished my shower with both eyes on the door. Years later a reporter told me about the man in the tux that was found having hung himself, and I was so freaked out that I cut the interview short, which I never do. It was chilling.

The thing is, though, that I did not get a sinister vibe off the thing. Tuxedo Man was just walking through my world (or I was just taking a shower in his) and probably did not even care that I was there. Our natural instinct as human/animal combos is to fear what we do not understand—the fight or flight method. But later, when we can rationalize and focus, we can see the true nature of things. My reaction was normal, as was my realization later that there was nothing to fear. Do not misunderstand: there have been times when I have experienced forces that *did* have ill intent, but Tuxedo Man was not one of those malicious beings. He was just having a stroll. Probably just wanted to see my overrated nakedness. There is nothing worse than a paranormal pervert.

Over the next few months the activity tripled. One of the boys swears he watched someone walk into his room, stand at the end of the bed . . . then slowly dissipate. He was sure it was one of us terrorizing him until the thing fucked off. After that he had a hard time even being in the room by himself. He moved all his shit out and waited until the very last minute to go to bed. Another ghost got into the machine in the control room one night as we were making a rough mix of "Vermilion"—it started looping a section of a verse, so we hit "record" and began making a remix of that loop. You can actually hear it on the album: it is in between "Before I Forget" and "Vermilion pt. 2."

Clown told me one that fucks with me to this day. Apparently he had gotten up one night to use the bathroom. As he was walking by my bed, he swore there was someone in the bed with me, squirming and moving around. When he switched the light on in the bathroom, he looked back and I was the only one there. No doubt you can see how this particular story made my blood curdle a bit. Meanwhile, more and more belongings were being flung about, and the screaming continued. A certain attic was exquisitely horrifying, emanating the sounds of a loud, violent murder for a full night. People started having serious talks about leaving, or at least swapping rooms.

The shenanigans in the Clown/Taylor wing kept on getting weirder and more irritating. Shit kept flying off of my roommate's dresser, no matter how many times he picked it up. One afternoon we were at the old music shop on La Cienega, Black Market Music (sadly no longer with us). We were looking for acoustic guitars; what we found were stacks of the same black-and-white photo of Robert F. Kennedy. So of course, because we are a clutch of quirks, we bought them all and displayed them in our rooms. But it was obvious from day one of this purchase that the "original" inhabitants of 2451 were not fans of RFK (bastard Republican haunts) and kept knocking them off of *everything*— walls, tables, whatever was being utilized.

I should explain that when we moved into the Mansion, there was no furniture or anything in the place. For Clown and me, we received two beds, two chests of drawers, two end tables, and two digital alarm clocks. Knowing Clown's love (read: pure white-hot hatred) for clocks in general, his remained on top of my bureau; mine was put on an end table, but I never bothered to set either of them, seeing as I got my time off of my nifty Nextel cell phone. The clocks were both wrong the entire time I was there; I never even thought about setting the alarms. So you can imagine my dismay when one night, at around 3:30 in the morning, *both* the alarms went off—at the same time, even though they were not synced up. Trust me—at that ungodly hour, I checked. There was no alarm, and there was no way they could have been on the same page, so to speak.

As I said before, the thermostat was in my room. This thermostat not only controlled the temperature in my room and Clown's little nook, but it also handled the temp for the entire second floor and subsequent wings on our side of the manse. Every morning I would put that thing on 70 degrees Fahrenheit. In sunny Los Angeles that is an acceptable and understandable setting; it could get hot as hell outside. I set it there so coming into the house felt nice and comfortable. Every morning I put it on 70, and within an hour the fucker would be on 85. Now I would still be in the room—no one was fucking touching it. But I would be working on lyrics, and suddenly I am making my own gravy, swimming in juices I never knew I had. I would jump out of bed—well, lazily slink out of bed, let's be fair—and run to the dial. There it was: 85 fucking degrees. No windows were open, and no doors were letting the cool air escape. The goddamned thing was being turned up, and nobody was around. This happened all the time, and it was driving me insane.

One night I was hanging out with friends in my room. Clown was off somewhere taking pictures or playing snare drums, so we had the place to ourselves. We were cracking each other up and taking pictures of each other doing goofy shit like sticking our guts out with our shirts pulled up and flexing like idiots, mugging for the camera with undisguised glee. I had the camera, and I was shooting around at other people when I noticed it was hot as fuck again. Jesus, what the hell? I got up off the bed, and sure enough, the bastard was locked in at 85 degrees. I had an uneasy notion, so for gits and shiggles, I went back through the photos I had been snapping, and one shot made me freeze and stare for a very long time. There, right next to my buddy being an idiot, were three orbs, swirling around and right on top of the thermostat. I still have the photo to this day. I shit you not. I showed everyone else in the room, and suddenly we felt the need to hang out somewhere else.

Another night I was sleeping soundly, dreaming about vampires or guns or whatever, when I woke up to music. Now you may be saying to yourself, "Of course you heard music, fuck hole—you were living in a recording studio." But the music I heard was not our music—hell, it was not even remotely close to Slipknot music. It was like old ballroom music, the kind you would hear at a dancehall or speakeasy in the twenties. It had a jaunty bounce to it, but it was lilting and hypnotic. And for some reason it was coming from my closet. I had a drowsy little moment when I was convinced someone had put a radio in there to fuck with me. Another crazy idea was that Sid (who essentially was holed up directly below my room) was doing some kind of soundtrack work for a period piece. Either way, I climbed slowly out of bed, opened the door . . . and it stopped dead. One minute there was a party going on, and the next there was cold, hard silence. I took a look around for a radio, but there was nothing there. The closet did not even have electrical outlets in it. I tried not to freak out, thinking I would get to the bottom of it in the morning. But when I got up the next day I found out there were only three people in the mansion that night. Then Sid hit me with a little chilling knowledge: "Nah, man. I was not playing music. I thought it was *you*. What the hell was that?" I left it at that and went back to eating M&Ms.

Let me tell you something really quick here: my time at the Mansion was not all spooks and specters. We had some really good times in that place, even if it was a little out of fucking control from time to time. There was one night when we threw a barbecue, and everybody and their mom showed up for it. It was so awesome that word spread down the Sunset Strip that "SLIPKNOT IS HAVING A FUCKING PARTY!" I remember standing on the veranda with an acoustic guitar. On one side was Sebastian Bach, singing madly and throwing monstrous high-fives at anyone within reach. On the other was B-Real from Cyprus Hill, who would not let me coax him into a stripped down rendition of "Insane in the Brain," no matter what I offered him. Behind me was a group of midge—er, dwarf—um, little people called Mini Kiss. And yes—they were in full Kiss makeup and costume.

This was the same night a certain actor who I will only refer to as Beak tried to get me to do crystal meth off a toilet on the second floor. I kindly refused. The night ended with me naked out on the patio, singing "Hard to Say Goodbye to Yesterday" by Boys II Men with four dudes I had never met before and have not seen since. Thankfully there is no video of this event, nor were they upset by my lack of pants. I woke up in my room (somehow), came downstairs to survey the damage, and nearly threw up when I realized I was the only one around who was going to clean the place. So I did: it took me nearly three fucking hours. Thanks, you prick cocksuckers.

I lived in the Mansion off and on for seven months. It had some incredible ups and unbelievable downs—remember, this was when I decided to give up my shitty whiskey-sodden lifestyle and get my shit together. But I look back with fondness on that time in my life. So mixed up in all the madness, there was the whisper of what was yet to come—and, better yet, what could be. I went through a serious life overhaul, and Slipknot got an amazing album out of the deal. On a humorous note, I broke my toe running up the main staircase one day, but not knowing I had broken it, I walked around on it for two and a half years before I finally had it x-rayed. It is still broken to this day; there is a pressure fracture on the main joint, making it swell up and turn red when I am on my feet for too long. The toenail filled with blood then died, causing it to grow irregularly. It is angry at all times, and it shakes when it senses evil. Yes, loyal readers and followers on Twitter . . . the Mansion was the place where Hugo the Angry Toe was born. He never sleeps. He never laughs. He just swells, hurts, and hates. I have learned over the years to never look Hugo in the eye. Those of you who follow me on various social networks have seen Hugo (I know I should apologize for posting pictures, but I do not give a rat's hairy ass). You have had a flash of my pain. Feel sorry for me.

The year 2003 turned to 2004, and I was preparing to leave the Mansion. We were making arrangements to finish the album at Rick Rubin's actual home, a place that is almost creepier than the house this chapter is dedicated to. Another band was getting ready to take over 2451, and I was setting up shop in a hotel. For one month I finished my vocals next to a giant stuffed bison I named Smitty in the basement of the Rubin residence. One night Trent Reznor showed up to hang out and see how things were going. Now, I am a *massive* Nine Inch Nails fan, so much so that when I heard Trent was there I could not even bring myself to go in the control room and meet him with everybody else. So while Joey, Paul, and our engineer, Greg Fidleman, sat chatting with him at the recording desk, I was out in the backyard that overlooked Sunset Boulevard pacing and chain smoking. From outside I heard the unmistakable strains of "The Blister Exists" being blasted from the studio's reference monitors inside. They were playing music for Trent! I wanted to go in and see what he thought, but I could not do it. When I finally got up the courage and walked inside, Trent was suddenly gone and everyone in the room was smiling. "What?" I said. They all looked at each other and Greg said, "Trent was fucking blown away. He said he had to go home. We think it fucked him up a bit!" When I finally met Trent years later, I asked him about it, and he simply laughed and nodded his head. I was very proud.

It was finally time to say goodbye and god bless to the hulking construct on Laurel Canyon. I was going to miss it in my own weird way. I had spent many nights really fucked up in that house. I had then started the long process of getting my shit to-gether halfway through my tenure there, swearing off drinking and devoting myself to being a better man all around. But before I moved out, there was one last happening that still gives me the chilly fucks to this day, ten years later. So do not say I did not warn you: proceed with caution, and a clean nappy.

My last night in my room I was alone because Clown had moved out and gone back to Iowa; he had finished his parts ear-lier and was spending time with his family before the tour fired up. When I looked at his side of our wing, it made me sad to see nothing over there—none of his posters, none of his . . . tobacco pipes, nothing but his rental furniture and a crude set of drapes to keep the California sun at bay. I could have used his balcony, but I never did—it still felt like his area, and I respected that, even though he was gone. I was almost done packing up the stuff I had accrued during my stay, like some posters, a broken acoustic guitar and a dock for my iPod so I could listen to music. My suitcases were stuffed to fits with all my clothes and toiletries. All I had to do was go to sleep, ship the stuff I would not take back home, and move into a hotel. In fact, that was the plan I fell asleep thinking about.

I am not sure what time it was when I saw the figure at the end of the bed.

I am quite sure it was between two and three in the morning, because the moonlight, which only shone in the window during those hours, was really bright for some reason. Then again, maybe this thing was creating this light. Either way, there was a pale blue-gray to the room, like that time in the morning when you know you should not be awake, but you have to pee, so you peep your eyes to slits and let your mind guide you toward the toilet like a telepath, praying to god you get there without stubbing your toes on the wall and also hoping you can keep yourself from pissing all over your feet. That was the color of the room. But there was also a dark shape right near my feet. As groggy as I was, I assumed it was one of the guys in the band, possibly looking for something or needing assistance. I was obviously in no mood to help with anything, so I closed my eyes again, if only for a split second.

That is when the covers were jerked violently off the bed and my already fairly chilly seminude frame. They were yanked so viciously that my body, which had hooked an arm around the top of the blankets and sheets in my slumber, was pulled up slightly from my waist to my chest. I rose up about half a foot and slammed back down. Well, needless to say, *that* fucking got my attention, and I shot awake with a start and a furious retort fully formed on my lips. Whoever was being a bleeding dick stain was going to face the full wrath of a delirious and vengeful Great Big Mouth.

There was nobody there. No one—not a fucking sausage. I was lying in my bed with no covers, angry and ready to fight *air*. I looked around the room; I even got out of bed and looked down the hallway. Most of the band had already gone home, so I am not sure who the hell I was looking for. My caveman brain was all fired up and wanted to scream at someone for waking me up and pissing me off. My logical brain could not get a handle on what had just happened. My body, meanwhile, was telling me to go back to sleep and we would be mad in the morning. So, being a man, that is just what I did. When I came to later and thought about the incident, I did what any man in my position would have done. I had a cup of coffee, got all my shit together, and got the *fuck* out of Dodge. I have not been back to the Mansion since.

In the years since, I have experienced more than my share of paranormal tomfoolery. As you will see later in this book, not only have I lived in places where not everything is what it seems, but I have actually consciously gone out of my way to find the things that go thump in the night. However, I regard those months spent in the Mansion as the most frightening and formative I have gone through since I was a child. It was invigorating and terrifying and absolutely out of fucking control at times. I not only ran the lanes on the edge faster than I had done since I was a teenager, but I had also been enveloped in a crazy world in which you were never sure if you were ever alone on any given night, whether the house was crammed full of people or not. These memories tantalize my taste for adventure from time to time, and I find myself looking back more frequently, even though it was the best of times and it was the worst of times, to paraphrase a man more savvy than myself. All I can tell you is that I am a different man from the one who moved into the Mansion back in the summer of 2003. That man may as well have died, his spirit roaming the halls and rooms of that house along with all the other beings who call 2451 Laurel Canyon a home away from home. That phase of my life was darkly appealing, but it served its purpose. So commingling with those shades of ghostly gray are all the things in life I let go of so I could be the man I am today. If there was such a thing as a baptism by Hell House, that wing of my memory palace is where it would be displayed. I know when I fall asleep tonight I will go back there because I have been typing about it and thinking about it. I am unafraid now. There is nothing that place can take from me ever again.

I work in Los Angeles all the time now, so it is nothing for me and my wife to go flying up around the crazy curves on Laurel Canyon on our way to the Burbank Airport or Travis Barker's studio or rehearsals for Camp Freddy or a plethora of other assignments I find myself embedded in on any given Sunday in the Sunshine State. Whether it is a charity event hosted by Henry Rollins or a private party sponsored by the people who make Rock Star video games, California is officially where I have crossed off several bucket list entries. From working with Dave Grohl to Halestorm, it all happens on the West Coast. I have definitely made peace with a lot of the demons in my life, some of which have permanent mailing addresses in that neck of the woods. But some habits will never change.

Every once in a while I find myself with some down time and an attitude. So you know what I do? I find Sunset Boulevard and turn up Laurel Canyon, heading toward the valley. I speed past Mt. Olympus (sort of). I twist and tweak around corners only a mentalist would love, ignoring the neighborhoods where all the rockers lived when they were busy reinventing rock and roll and swiftly making my way toward the general store on the corner where the groupies used to go beg for superstar penis. I floor it through the intersection of Laurel Canyon and Lookout Mountain until I see the familiar obscured corner with the trees and the fence and the entryway that never gets used. I slow down for about half a block, spit out the window, and extend my favorite filthy bit of single-fingered sign language. Quick: watch what I do from the right side of the car to the cottage on the left.

You just saw me flip the bird at a haunted house.

ONE NIGHT IN FARRAR

HE NEXT SERIES OF PAGES are no shit, holy fuck, by the book, documented and completely bloody true. This is the result of hours spent on the job and in the thick of it, running around in the dark and nearly pissing myself. If you feel like you cannot get behind that, well tough titty fat. Besides, I have the tapes to prove it. So suck it . . . or at least throw a little powder on it. Better get a pot of coffee, because we are officially about to get weird.

For some of the chapters held within, my intention was to go out on some bona fide ghost hunts, recording and writing what I saw and experienced (no matter what that was) so I could have some fresh material. I have been exposed to several paranormal phenomena, even in my own home, but I wanted to spread the love. I wanted new haunts. I wanted to wander around abandoned buildings and houses like I did when I was ten years old. I love being scared, even if I know perfectly well that there is no reason to *be* scared. The sensation is overwhelming; it is the closest to coming unhinged as I allow. So when I feel it, I revel in it as much as inhumanly possible. It was time to get out of my own head and into the night.

Nothing gets the blood going like pure adventure. Every step you take out of your comfort zone gets you closer to the action of life. Too many people lean into their armchairs and watch from the cheap seats when they could be charging in, getting among it, doing the deeds that get you headlines and legendary status. There is a time and a place for complacency; there is also a time when you get your ass out of that divot in the sofa and treat life more like an amusement park than a parking lot. Nothing kills the spirit of action and excitement more than the need to take a nap after Thanksgiving dinner. Then again, if you pile on too much turkey, you miss the big game anyway. Sometimes the only way to pick up the pace is to pace yourself so you have enough energy for the home stretch. Let those show-offs run ahead and waste their energy. Stamina will always beat arrogance in the end.

So I made plans to make some myths. But in order to pull off the great escape, I knew I could not go alone. I was going to need a team . . . or at least a bunch of friends willing to sit in near dark all night without complaining much. I needed a crack squad of miscreants steady of hand or paw, equipped with nerves of steel and night-vision cameras. I needed allies and night owls with tons of patience but a penchant for the verbose. In other words, I needed a bunch of people with the night off and no plans for Crisco Twister. So I went about the business of assembling my misfit band of Avengers Lite . . . and assemble they did.

My wife: code-name "The Boss." Her superpower is a near Hulk-like strength and an uncanny sixth, seventh, and eighth sense for sniffing out bullshit like a fart in a cockpit. My wife was going to be the anchor of the team, the feather in the flaws. Having absolute trust in her ability to feel when something is going to happen, she would handle leadership when our people split up for exploration. She could also limit the amount of damage we would do, as the rest of the group was akin to swinging a baseball bat in a crystal shop.

Matt: code-name "Stubs." Stubs is the member with the most experience going on these misadventures. He would be our tech specialist, making sure we were using the right gear—that is, digital cameras, audio recorders, flashlights, and so forth. Being that he is the man with the most hair, I made an executive decision to disallow any use of candles during our surveillance. He also has a never-ending reservoir of sadism that manifests in tormenting the next person on our list.

Lauren: code-name "Lady." Lady is what we will call "the divining rod" for the expedition. In other words, she is terrified of what we are going to do, what we are going to see, and what we are going to put her through. She has a propensity for screaming, running, and shaking uncontrollably. Quite frankly, it is fucking hilarious to freak her out. She is also one of the sweetest people I have ever known, which makes me feel bad about torturing her as much as we do, though I am sorry to say that bad feeling is very short-lived.

Chris: code-name "Big Truck." Truck is exactly like his nickname implies—a man the size of a fucking truck. Trust me—think "Mack" more than "Ram." He is also a novice to this whole "ghost hunting" thing. But his enthusiasm for the project made him an obvious choice. Killjoys can suck the fun out of an auditorium, and I have no room on this squad for dick bags. At the end of the day, believe what you want. Just do not get your peanut brittle on my chocolate. So Truck was invited for his exuberance . . . and his high-end camera.

Kennedy: code-name "Kennedy." Kennedy is the king of what they call in sports entertainment "color commentary." If there is a quip to be made, Kennedy will jump off a cliff to get to it first. That is what I want from him—the line that no one else could come up with. Oh, and he also has a sick addiction to scaring the fuck out of Lady. So he and Stubs will be perfect teammates together. The benefit of this setup is even if we are not able to get any evidence, it will still be ridiculous.

First, though, I needed some locations. In Iowa alone there are several famous or infamous destinations with purported "paranormal activity." The most famous of these is the Axe Murder House in Villisca. An hour and a half outside of Des Moines, it has enjoyed national notoriety for over one hundred years.

Sometime in the wee hours of June 10, 1912, eight people were found bludgeoned and axed to death in the home of Josiah Moore, including Josiah, his wife, Sarah, their children, and two young visitors who were staying the night. It is one of the earliest examples of mass murder and psychotic criminal pathology in American history. It is also one of the most grisly unsolved murders ever. Over the years the ghastly ghostly goings-on have made this place a haunted hot spot for aficionados around the world: things fly about, screams cry out, children laugh and shriek in horror, and so forth. A friend even told me about being hit in the face with a tennis ball he was fucking about with Great Escape style. He was hit so hard, in fact, that it bloodied his nose. He almost broke his ankle fleeing the place.

It had everything I wanted in a ghost hunt. It was perfect.

It is also almost always completely booked full pretty much year round—no open reservations, much to my chagrin. I even dropped my name—to which they replied, "Corey who?" Never let it be said that an attempt at using fame to your advantage can bite you in the ass from time to time.

SO! I turned my attention to an old school building thirty minutes from my front door.

In 1919 the Washington Township Consolidated School District was established, and three years later a schoolhouse was opened in Farrar, Iowa, that would cater to kindergarten through twelfth grade. Many of the local rural towns and counties utilized it until it closed in 2002 after eighty years of service. Then it sat for five years abandoned. In 2007 Jim and Nancy Oliver purchased it, hoping to make it a unique home while also restoring the old girl to its original luster. However, even before the couple took up residence, tales of strange goings-on had persisted for years. When they eventually moved in, they found they were not alone. Orbs darted about. Shadow people ran amok. Voices could be clearly heard everywhere. Small children were seen in the stairways before they would vanish without a trace. Nancy Oliver herself was steadied on a staircase when she nearly fell. Turning to thank her husband, whom she assumed was the one who had given her the helping hand, she found herself standing alone.

After reading all this, the place definitely had potential. I also liked the fact that it was not very well known. It was not one of the common names that you see when you look up a list of "popular haunts," like the Stanley Hotel in Colorado or the Amityville House (whichever one that is; it is widely believed that was a hoax). But something was bothering me. All the research I had done did not uncover one tidbit of evidence to explain why the place was experiencing this activity. With all the reports dating back to when the school was open, it was apparent this had been going on for a really long time, but why? For all intents and purposes, it seemed like a wholesome, friendly little establishment for that township, steeped in tradition and beloved by those who had called it their place of education. But nothing was reported involving a dark side—not even a crumb of violence. What had happened there, or what was connected to the site and was keeping it there?

I prepared for metaphysical battle.

Actually, I bought some digital recorders, appropriated some night-vision cameras, and made sure to bring a chair. And flashlights—oh my, did we have some flashlights! The Boss has an extensive collection of them and allowed me to borrow one of her high-end flashlights: a black Scorpion that she said could be dropped from the roof and would not break. I have been told that it always pays to be prepared. Honestly, I have never ever been paid for being prepared; I have been assured of payment, but there was never cash on delivery. But it never hurts to be ahead of the curve, so I scuttled about gathering these accoutrements. I grabbed a sweatshirt too—you know . . . because it gets cold.

Yeah, I get cold.

I am *not* a wuss.

Oh, fuck you.

We drove out in two vehicles, following directions that could only be understood in Iowa: "Well, when you get to the *first* distressed and decrepit grain silo, you are close. If you pass the *second* distressed and decrepit grain silo, you have gone too far . . ." As we rode along, the mood was loose and fun. The sky was doing some crazy shit, though. The colors looked like something out of a horror movie when the editors are finished with post-production. But we passed the time by concocting terrible pranks to play on Lady, who was riding in the other car and had no idea what we were planning. We were wrapping our minds around the adventure that lay before us. Stubs was also using a fancy Internet website to call Lady from phone numbers that could not be recognized, taunting her with scary silences when she answered her phone and leaving terrifyingly cryptic messages in her voicemail when she ignored his calls. The one I liked the most was when he let her sit in silence for several seconds, then muttered, "Whatever you do, do not look in the glove compartment." She screamed something fairly cross and vulgar into the phone and promptly hung up on him.

Just as the excitement was making us giggle like mad people, we were there.

Taking a left at a quaint country church, we turned off the highway and found the schoolhouse set back on a plot a little off the road. Across the street was a family home and a cemetery that seemed to hold most of the old residents for a twenty-mile radius. The Olivers had hired a caretaker named Steve, who met us at the door and showed us to what he called the Safe Room. It turned out to be the old faculty lounge, with a TV, some couches, and a refrigerator. For a second, dragging a cooler and all those chairs along with us seemed redundant, but then I realized that if we had not brought those things, none of this comfort would have been there. So says the Laws of Murphy, anyway . . .

A few of us ventured across the street to the tiny rustic cemetery, and judging from the headstones, it had been there a long time—some of them dated back to the mid-1800s. It was no bigger than an average backyard in a city suburb, but the stones were ancient and the names barely legible from seasons of weathering the elements. As I strolled the rows, the names appeared to be a little clearer, and suddenly it occurred to me that I recognized almost every name here. I had come across these names in my research—here laid the family who had owned the land and had given it to the county. Here were the names of various faculty members and students. Here were the people who had grown up and died with this wonderfully unassuming school as the heart of this close-knit community. I had a strange feeling; I was about to trounce around the center of their universe. Even if they were no longer around, this was still their place. I was the trespasser, the transgressor. Was I spitting in their pool, laughing in the face of their heritage? I did my best to fill my mind with positive thoughts. I was not here to condescend; I was here to observe.

Steve offered to give us a tour but cautioned against it, saying that the feedback from other groups had told him that the activity doubled if people were not led around beforehand and that the experiences might be skewed if our forethought was saddled with preconception. So we decided to bypass the tour, thanking Steve for his time and accompanying him out the front door (the only exit that did not lock you out when it closed behind you) so we could have one more smoke prior to our first bit of exploration around the school. After extinguishing our cigarettes, we ventured back to the Safe Room to grab our gear and take a look around.

The first pass of the site was like being ten years old on a field trip to a museum. It seemed like every room had remnants of the building's old life in it. Notebooks sat in empty filing cabinets, desks were shoved into corners or overturned completely, old pictures adorned corkboard above giant tears in the walls where people had come in to take whatever blackboards could be procured, and books from the past fifty years were shoved into the backs of cupboards to be discovered later like treasures in a killer's house. The whole place had the feeling of mass exodus, like it had been abandoned during an air raid or an attack by a tornado. In turn, it made you feel like you should flee as well. But overall there was no malice in the air like I had felt in other places. As uncomfortable as it became later in the evening and in the early morning hours, the school never had the feeling like we were in danger, like it did not want us there. Maybe that is why we stayed as long as we did, even after all the weirdness started happening later on.

The layout was not very confusing. The school is three stories tall—four if you count the slightly below-ground gymnasium. Walking in the front door, you are confronted with two choices: upstairs to the second floor or through a pair of entries to the ground level that overlooks the gym. Through the gym and to the left is the boiler room; to the right are the only working toilets we could use. Each floor above had six classrooms and respective boys' and girls' restrooms. On the third floor were the principal's office and a diminutive auditorium we started referring to as the Theater Room. We found the old kitchen, which had a really loud dumbwaiter and some hastily stored office supplies, but the floor seemed to be falling through in places, so we decided we would not spend a lot of time wandering around in a room where the ground could breach at any moment. As we made our way upward to the various levels, nothing was triggering our inner Venkman—that is, until we got to the boys' bathroom on the second floor. Everyone who explored that room came away with a sickened vibe we could not put our finger on. It was pretty obvious something bad had gone down in there. I earmarked it for its own recording device and continued the preliminary walkabout.

After we were done we returned to the Safe Room for a quick snack and a chance to go over our initial impressions. Lady was excited, scared, but not uncomfortable. The Boss voiced what we all felt: this was not the site of a murder, but there was something not right, especially in that bathroom, where the ominous feeling had an emotional odor to it. Kennedy was still reserving judgment. Stubs was anxious to set up the equipment. Truck was just taking it all in. I was not sure what to think, but I knew it was time to get cracking. So we finished our snacks and plotted where we would plant our devices. One audio recorder would go in the second-floor bathroom where we all felt sick. One camera would go in the gymnasium, overlooking the entire room. Another camera would go in one of the classrooms that had given Kennedy a hinky feeling. Meanwhile, we would break up into pairs with recorders and cameras and roam, looking to engage whatever we could and try to pick up either EVPs or actual visual instances. We were finally here. The time for talk and speculation was over—it was time to get to work.

Kennedy and I started in the Theater Room, sitting on the stage in a booth I am fairly certain I last saw in an old A&W restaurant miles away. I do not know why it was on the stage or how it got there, but it was comfy and we could face each other. Meanwhile, Lady and The Boss were doing quick sweeps of some of the other rooms on that floor and the one below. Truck and Stubs were down in the boiler room by the gym. The silence was so thick that I started to think I had tinnitus. Other than the near-complete blackout, it was kind of relaxing. It was hot and smelled like a million kindergarteners had left their soiled undies in the ceiling tiles somewhere, but it was not too bad. Trust me—I have been in worse places. I once spent a night in a hotel room in Italy that reeked of dead hookers and strawberries. I could not check out of that place fast enough. The strange thing was that it had great wi-fi.

I was doing some EVP work with Kennedy. For those of you unfamiliar with the term, it stands for "Electronic Voice Phenomena." The human voice only registers at a certain frequency or megahertz. EVPs are supposedly sounds or voices outside those parameters that can be picked up with recorders. Basically, he and I were asking questions and sitting in silence, trying to allow time and space for an answer that we may or may not hear with the naked ear. We had been sitting there for a while, asking random questions and hoping we could illicit a response, when we both heard what was either crying, laughing, or moaning. We looked at each other and listened intently, hoping to discern if it was our compatriots or something we could not explain. We decided it might have been a dog, but we filed it away for further discussion later.

This is how it went for a while: sitting in rooms, asking questions to the night that had very little hope of being answered right away. As we went outside for another round of smokes, we talked about ways to beat the ennui. Stubs thought it would be a good idea to chain Lady up and leave her in the boiler room. He could not understand why she did not share his sentiment. We finally agreed on doing some EVP work in the Theater Room together. We went inside and moved some of the recording equipment around to different rooms, making sure to say that we were doing so aloud so it was documented properly. I went to another classroom to try an experiment: I set up some toy cars in an attempt to possibly broker some movement out of whatever was running around the place. Truck must have had the same idea, because he entered another room and opened one of the file cabinets to see if something would happen to it. Then we set up shop in the Theater Room, sitting in a circle in front of the stage like some bizarre campfire round robin.

You might want to grab your popcorn, because this is where it gets interesting.

It started with The Boss, who, as I said before, has an extra sense for these things, hearing singing. She described a little boy somewhere in the complex singing the "Pledge of Allegiance," sort of showing off for us like children are prone to do. Every once in a while some of us could pick up on it a bit. The Boss could hear it plain as day, though. Suddenly, she shot up out of her seat and said, "What room is across the hall to the left by the stairs?" It was a classroom Kennedy and I had been inside while we were moving around the other recorders. We all grabbed our flashlights and, like some bizarre wayward football huddle, we moved in that direction.

There had been an encyclopedia sitting on the windowsill in that room when we were there, and the floor was clean. As we entered, the first thing I noticed were torn pages—*torn pages*—lying on the floor across the room from where that book was still sitting, now open and rent asunder. No windows were open and we were the only people around. Someone had torn pages out of this book and strewn them all over the place. We sat there, listening intently. The Boss was trying to get the little boy's name. We all held our breath. The lack of sound was suffocating. So you can imagine our reaction when, from somewhere far below us, deep in the school, we heard a crash of metal on metal that was loud enough to make Lady cry out.

Like something out of a scene from the movie *Clue,* we all shot through the hallways and down the stairs to the room in question. At first we could not figure out what had made that horrendous noise. Then Truck calmly stated, "That file cabinet was open when I went upstairs." He had opened it as a sort of test before we had corralled ourselves in the Theater Room. We looked: all the drawers were closed. When I yanked on it myself, the damn thing had been slammed shut so hard I had to jerk it to get it open. There was much conjecture and running of scenarios, but we all agreed that even if there had been a window open, the wind could not have shoved that thing back in. The rusty resistance was too strong. Someone had to have pushed it shut . . . hard.

We returned to our circle of trust, discussing everything excitedly. Stubs and I wondered if we were experiencing things now because we were ignoring it—before we were kind of chasing favor and got nothing. Now, though, we were paying more attention to each other, so the activity felt a little like "pay attention to me!" So it made sense to continue that approach: let it come to us and not the other way around. We repositioned the recorders and some of us went outside for a smoke while the others stayed behind to listen and watch. I was enjoying the chill and inhaling the smoke when I could have sworn I saw something in the trees around the corner from where we stood. I did not have time to explore that too much. A light came on in one of the rooms, and we were fairly certain none of our people were in there. Kennedy ran inside to check. The group who had stayed behind was right where we had left them, and a further search of the room in question left us scratching our heads.

As we finished our carcinogens, a car pulled up. It was our friends Biff and Knees (well, of *course* these are codenames—who would name their child Knees?). I did not want to give them too much info, seeing as I wanted a righteous judgment about the place. So I chose to wait to fill them in on everything until after they had gotten a feel for the surroundings. They were greatly intrigued and very excited—a couple beers imbibed on their part probably did not hurt their states of mind either. But I was not too worried about that.

I guided Biff and Knees through the hallways, showing them the rooms and the layout but not going into detail about anything other than the history. We were down in the lower section by the gymnasium. I was holding one of the double doors open for them to come through so we could descend the stairs down to see the boiler room. I heard something like movement through air, and Knees let out a yell. Biff and I turned to see what the trouble was, and he said, "Something just ran past me and stepped on my foot!" I scanned back down the hallway only to see nothing. Knees shook it off, and we laughed as we went to see the rest of the building. After we finished the brief tour we grabbed some more chairs and went back to find our friends to reassemble our kinetic circle for some chitchat.

Just outside the door to the Theater Room in the hallway I had set up a recorder on a chair. From my vantage point I could see the red light on the device, letting me know it was still on. This turned out to be terribly handy. While we were all sitting around talking about past experiences, I noticed out of the corner of my eye that something was constantly blocking that red light. I started tuning everyone out and shifted my focus to the doorway. Sure enough, I saw something peeking around the corner at me several times. Stubs saw it too. It was like a spooky version of *Catch Me If You Can.* Just as we were all turning our attention to the doorway, we heard something in the room immediately behind us. There was a door that connected the two rooms, and as we stepped into it, I heard laughter in the hallway. Spine-tingling stuff, but I was starting to feel something else. I know I am (supposedly) a big, strong badass man and everything. Even so, I was frustrated; this was getting ridiculous, and not for nothing I wanted to kick that little shit's ass.

Meanwhile, the temperature in the Theater Room was starting to get schizophrenic. One moment it would be nice and cozy, and seconds later it would be stiflingly uncomfortable. Sweat ran from our faces and then suddenly dried as it cooled. So we walked around some more. I took Biff and Knees to that bathroom where we had all felt physically ill. As we stood in the dark, around a corner by the stalls Biff whispered, "I think I am going to throw up." I could feel her pain; this was a type of porcelain hell, draped in art deco and painted with some sort of unnatural misery. What the hell could have happened in there? I started looking at how the restroom was designed.

As you walked through the door you could go to the right to one set of stalls and urinals, or you could go to the left with an entirely different set of both. There was one catch: if you went to the left, one of the stalls cut off the rest of the room. But if you went to the right, you could keep going around by the window. I discovered there was a two-person sized nook back in the corner, hidden from view. It suddenly occurred to me that it was the perfect place for an attack. The layout was almost ripe for a sexual assault; no one would see anything from the doorway if they entered. My mind twisted that over and over like an equation. Was that why it was borderline unbearable in that bathroom? If so, who was victim and who was predator? Mind you, I have not one shred of evidence—this is all hypothesis. But I know what I am talking about. I have been on the dangerous end of that type of business. I recognized the feeling in my chest from standing in that room. I knew it all too well. Something very bad had happened in there, and though I was not sure exactly what that thing was, I knew it like I know the sound of rain and the feel of fire.

I took my friends and got out of there. We did some more walking around and some more EVP work, trying to chase down as many actions as we could. But the night was winding down. We decided to do one more round of the place. Everyone else went down to the first floor. The Boss and I stayed upstairs. We were in one of the classrooms talking and trying to coax a little more from our childlike visitor. Suddenly we heard whistling in the hall. We assumed it was the others and continued our conversation. But then we heard the others coming up the stairs— on the other side of the school. When they came to our room, they asked *us* if we had been whistling. We said we had thought they were the ones doing it. Luckily, there had been a camera set up in the hallway, shooting down to capture any movement. We rewound to the spot. Sure enough, with no one around, an un-settling bit of whistling began to lilt through the air. It made me excited to check what we had gathered that night. It was also the perfect capper for the evening.

It was 2 a.m. Even though we had the building until seven that morning, we were all tired and longing for our beds. So we began packing up and getting our shit ready to take it all home. We crawled into our vehicles for the trip. You can imagine the dichotomy: these adventurous scamps who had been so eager to see what the old madam had to offer, now so obviously ex-hausted that most of us fell asleep in the car before we got back to the two-lane highway that led the way back to the hearth. Our curiosity sated, we fell in between the sane and slumber, minds racing for the close embrace of sleep while cataloging our vari-ous encounters. Nuff said, as Stan Lee put it. Shut the machines down and recharge.

It was a few weeks before I was able to sit down and sift through the hours of footage and audio tracks to see what I could find, helped along with a healthy dose of coffee, smokes, and quiet. There were all the cameras in the halls and the gym, the audio recorders set in the various classrooms and bathrooms, and the handheld recorders we were all carrying around with us. Let me tell you: the only thing more boring than reading and recording your own audio book is sitting, watching, waiting, and listening to hours of content in the hopes of capturing something fantastic. Some shit did not even show up—there were various tracks that failed to record for some reason. Listening back, I could hear voices complaining that the power kept draining in the batteries. So some of the evidence did not get captured. Note to self: next time plug the shit into a wall socket. Of the stuff that was recorded, there are several conversations of past experiences that I will tell you about later on in the book. There are hours of nothing. There are noises from outside and squeaking wood—the floors in the Theater Room were especially peculiar sounding. It gave me the impression of breathing, somewhere between Darth Vader and Bane. So my investigation was moving in fits and starts, from silence to silly quips.

That was until I found something that could not be explained.

In some of the rooms, out of nowhere, the recorders picked up soft humming. This was not electric in any way; this was musical, the sound of a child walking around with a song stuck in his or her head. It showed up on several different recorders, almost like this kid was casually strolling through the halls from room to room singing for anyone who could hear. It made me wonder if this was the kid that The Boss heard when we were sitting around in a circle. I also found breathing in the boys' bathroom where we all felt sick. This was a recorder we had set up and left to see what we could get. The breathing appears hours after anyone has been in there. It starts, lasts a few seconds, and then it just stops. It is another thirty minutes before anyone comes in, and his or her presence is announced and punctuated by the heavy door opening and slamming shut.

The stuff that we witnessed and heard is also there: the file cabinet slamming shut is heard on several devices. More chilling was the shape I caught on one of the cameras. Upstairs, in what used to be the principal's office, a shape blocks one of the lights for a full ten seconds, and then you can see it move away to the left. It disappeared into a storage closet that has no exit and nothing comes out the entire time afterward. Of course, there are things that can be explained right away. The moaning or crying that Kennedy and I heard most assuredly was a dog howling outside. There are whines that slowly materialize into car engines.

Nine times out of ten, footsteps turn out to be Stubs—that boy has the heaviest feet of any person alive; he sounds like Frankenstein rolling out for a morning jog. There is a glorious moment on one of the devices when someone—and I will not say who—is sitting in a room alone and they cut one of the raunchiest farts known to all recorded history. This was a Roman fart, a fart that could conquer territories and topple governments. It was fucking funnier than hell and was made even more hilarious because that person not only says "excuse me" to no one in particular, but they also start to giggle uncontrollably. Someone else ends up coming in the room, and they must have gotten a whiff, because you hear a quiet little "what the fuck . . . ?" and the perpetrator loses control altogether. I laughed out loud myself when I came to that bit. It made my fucking night.

My analysis for the Farrar schoolhouse is simple but complicated, to say the least. I believe something is there. But I also believe that it has nothing to do with a murder or a death. I just think this building has become a home, a safe place, for a wayward spirit. I will explain it like this: aside from the dark feeling we felt in that second-floor bathroom, none of us had the impression that something bad had happened in that building. There is something to be said about that, because many people can really tell when a location has that kind of sinister feeling—places like Dachau and Neely Plaza in Dallas have those vibes, like the violent events cause something to change in the very environment, giving it an edge and a sadness that was not there before. My team did not feel that anywhere other than that bathroom. So my opinion is that, yes, there is something there, but it could easily be a spirit who resides in the cemetery across the street and has returned to the schoolhouse because that was where it was the happiest. It could also be the spirit of the child who had something happen in that bathroom and that torment has tied it inexplicably to this building in the middle of nowhere. It could be a shadow of someone's life, like a teacher who both attended and taught at the school and returned because so much of their life was spent treading those hallways. Who knows, really? To me, it would most likely take someone from that same time to find out exactly who or what that person is and why its soul has chosen this place to replay and relive its days. I may never know, and quite frankly it will not cause me to lose sleep. But someone has that knowledge. Who knows if that question will ever be answered to the best of our abilities?

As I sit here months later thinking about it, I am struck by several notions. That schoolhouse felt like it had a personality unto itself. The more we spent time in it, the more we got to know it and to appreciate the adventures and the experiences beheld during our stay there. I remember walking around outside by myself, getting the lay of the land and just taking it all in. The sky still had that ominous hue about it, and all the playground equipment was rusty and dark, threatening us more with tetanus than anything resembling a good time. The trees around the place definitely helped set the mood; their limbs hung low around your head like hands reaching for fistfuls of your hair, wanting to drag you up into their leaves and digest you at their leisure. So maybe these factors set the tone for that evening and the things we felt and saw. But I consider myself to be a fairly intelligent and levelheaded chap; I do not panic easily and I do not run from danger or the unexpected. All I really know is that I have a handful of memories that I share in some way with the people I was there with, and we were all involved. Make your own mind up as far as I am concerned.

Some people might say we wanted to find something there. Others might say we left before anything else fascinating could happen. This debate will rage long after I am finished typing it up—who saw what and what was real, and so on. Personally, I feel like these rich visions are what they appear to be: a collision of data and stimuli that occurred in an environment to instill belief and satisfactory contemplation. You can try to figure it out all you want, like dissecting a magic trick behind the master's back. You can twist it around forever, and maybe you will have varying conclusions each time. But those are rare privileges for the ones who did not make the journey. For those who stood watch and tested our mettle, we know the score better than the team who was playing. It is a matter of knowing and believing, like I have said before. I know because I was there. You can believe what you want, but because you were absent on the day in question, I rest my case gladly.

I guess the best way to tie this all up is to tell you about the last bit of evidence I found in the Farrar files. Here is the scene: we had all been camped in the Theater Room talking. After a while we all decided we needed to smoke our asses off again (like we ever needed any convincing), so we left the room. Kennedy stayed behind, quietly sitting and listening for anything that we might miss. The recorder was in the middle of the room, and it picked up our exit. For ten minutes there is nothing but Kennedy's breathing. Finally, he says out loud, "Well, I think I am going to go outside with everyone else. We might be gone for a little bit, so if there is anything you want to say or do before I go, here is your chance. Can you make a noise, or a sound, or anything?" Silence reigned. You eventually hear Kennedy stand up and head toward the door, saying, "Well, it was worth a shot .

. ." The words trail away, falling into silence, along with his footsteps. The room is left empty. It is very obvious that no one is in the room.

Out of nowhere, something knocks on a metal folding chair three times.

PARANORMAL, PARALYSIS and PARANOID PARAMETERS

SPOILER ALERT: this chapter is full of fantastic claims, biting commentary, and other things that will piss off cynics, atheists, and malcontents alike. It has a bunch of nonsense known as "scientific law" and other shit known simply as "the great halls of my memory palace." Some of you might actually— dare I say it—*learn* something in this chapter that you may not have been privy to before you bought this foul piece of wood pulp. So my condolences to those of you who pride yourself on "keeping it real" or running your life according to horse pucky you picked up on the Bravo Network. Their motto is "Watch What Happens"—the only problem is that when you do watch what happens, you end up dumber than a bag of brand new hammers. So this chapter is full of shit that might make you smarter, even if the conjecture on my part turns out to be ridiculous and implausible. I warned you. Read with a helmet and at your own discretion.

Numbers have always interested me. I love rhythms and figures and calculations. Even though I am a very right-brained fellow, I have this bizarre left-brain bend that is fascinated with statistics, math, and symmetry. I have explained in other forms of literary drivel that I am obsessed with even numbers. This transfers to everything in my life. I can only chew pieces of gum in even numbers: two, four, or, in the case of long commercial flights where smoking is not an option, eight. This permeates my adult life like a phantom waiting to snatch the girl at the end of her sonata. I do not know why and I cannot help it—even therapy would have no affect on this tendency, or as my wife The Boss calls it, "my cute little neurosis." That's fine: she has the same thing with odd numbers—detests the number three. I think that shit is funny. I will also be sleeping on the couch for a while, seeing as I just told you all about it.

The minutia of datum, facts, and figures—these things envelop my screaming id and give me a sense of stability, a grounded line in all this faulty wiring. I become engrossed in finding a solution instantly, causing many people to ask me "if I am all right" and members of my own family to question whether or not I am psychotic. I get absorbed in different ideas and solving problems, losing all concepts of time and presence to the point at which, when I come to, I find I have not shaved, I am missing my pants, and I am stranded at a bus station somewhere in New Mexico. Jesus, if I had a nickel for every time I was stranded at a bus station in New Mexico . . .

Maybe it is because I like to grab hold of the structure of any given concept, to get a grip on it and therefore some understanding. As lovely as chaos can be sometimes, especially when you are stranded at a bus station in New Mexico, to me order is the warm blanket waiting for you when you get home, along with a cup of coffee and the sports page. Chaos has no meaning without order and vice versa; there is no basis for relativity when there is nothing to use for comparison. A clean house is always going to look cleaner if the place next door is Hoarder's Hideaway, but you would not know it if the two were not sitting right next to each other. So chaos and order are necessary bedfellows, allowing freaks like me to embrace both and hop to and from each individual bouncy castle whenever the mood takes me.

Anyway, while I was researching this book I wanted to get a feel for where the national and international psyches are on the subject of the paranormal. Obviously, movies like *Paranormal Activity* and shows like *Ghost Hunters* have given even the most ardent skeptics a moment of pause and have heightened our awareness. But I wanted to know how many hombres and fillies in the herd of the Earth were on the spooky schooner with me.

So I surfed around the Net gathering data on the subject. You know what I found out? Either people are more fucked than I thought or the minds behind these surveys are sitting in their own toiled soil, so to speak.

On average, it seems 48 percent of people believe in the existence of ghosts. This is based on several websites I traversed, including wiki.answers.com. That being said, this is the Internet we are talking about, and the same website said that 62 percent of people are skeptical of the existence of ghosts. I am not a doctor, but even I can add: 48 plus 62 is 110. You cannot have 110 percent in a survey. What are you saying—that most people believe in ghosts *and* most people deny their existence? You cannot have more than one most. Your choices are none, some, more, most, and all—end of list. Even if you use the phrase "more than most," it still does not make any fucking sense. By the way, there is another word for the phrase "more than most": it is called "all."

So half the population believes in ghosts, if you believe the skewed numbers on this site and others. According to the same poll, 22 percent of those people have had an actual experience or a sighting. Another poll says that most of the people who do not believe in ghosts are over the age of sixty-five. That right there says a lot to me. Does it mean that the younger generation is more open-minded? Does it mean that the older generation will rationalize away altercations when they can? I will not allow an assumption on my part, but I can say this: I know more young people who are Democrats than are Republicans, and of those young Republicans, most of the ones I know refer to themselves as conservatives. They agree with my notion that "the R word" carries the stigma of ignorance, bigotry, and stubborn prejudices, not to mention the airs of the upper 1 percent. The same can be said for racism and the attitudes toward civil rights. So there is a tendency for the young to weed out and let go of tired philosophies.

I think it is safe to say I have established that not only do I believe in the existence of spirits, but I also am unabashedly realistic about my experiences. I am not going to sit here and tell you I believe in shit like magic, although there was a guy I met backstage once who had some serious tricks up his sleeve. How do you manage to get the card I chose from the deck into my back pocket? That is some Merlin shit right there—to this day I check my underwear before I take a shower to make sure I do not have an eight of spades stuffed in my male box. There is nothing worse than cleaning soggy tattered bits of paper out of your can. Shit, where was I?

Even though I have no doctorates or degrees, I have some theories, scientific conjecture, and intelligent guesses. Some other people might have already made these suppositions, but these are things I have been thinking about for a long time— honestly since I was old enough to start putting two and two together, which I believe still equals four. I know—I am not just another pretty face. In fact, I have several pretty faces that I keep in a box in the basement. I only wish I could remember their names.

I did it again, huh? Sorry—I distract easily.

To me, spirits are energy. Thanks to *The Matrix,* I understand now that the human body produces enough energy to power a world of deadly machines. We are 9-volts with two legs and a hunger for bacon. I would be remiss if I did not posit the theory that the human soul makes up a lot of that energy. That kind of represents a major chunk of my case. Yeah, I know what you are thinking: "Jesus wept, is he going to hit us with some schoolhouse shit?" The answer, my friend, is you bet your ass I am. In fact, I am going to break it down for you as well. Peter Griffin once said, "Some words are long and hard to understand." Well, I apologize, but I am going to throw some polysyllabic information at you so you can see where I am coming from. Hey, let's be honest: some of you might need it to keep up! In this day and age, when some girls have no idea they are pregnant and most guys cannot even be bothered to wash their balls, I think explaining myself should be par for the course. So here goes.

I said before that my belief is that the human soul makes up the majority of the energy we emit from our bodies. Then again, maybe it is the energy of the body that provides fuel and nourishment for the development of the soul. Either way it serves this idea. Warning: the following is fairly educational. If you are allergic to things like learning and thinking, it would be best if you brought in what they would refer to in baseball as a "pinch reader." The next few paragraphs are loaded with science. I know I gave you a heads up earlier, but I am certain you all thought I was just tossing a load of bollocks at your face. No, I meant that shit—there is some actual learned shit going on here! Anyway, it is what it is. Sorry if you mistakenly leave here with some unwanted knowledge; it was truly not my intention. Everyone got his or her beakers, goggles, and adult pants on? Yes? Then we shall begin.

According to the first law of thermodynamics—more specifically, its first principle, known as the law of conservation of energy—"energy can neither be created nor destroyed." It goes on to say that "energy can change forms and it can flow from one place to another, but the total energy of an isolated system remains the same." So put that in perspective with the existence of ghosts and the concept of reincarnation. If we exude and are made up of energy and that law is true, where does that energy go after we die? Does it search out another system, that is, a new life form preparing to surface in this world? Or do they linger in a place they understand but cannot reenter the way they did before? What if ghosts are pure human energy? And how can scientists flat-out deny their existence and not take all these variables into consideration?

What if ghosts are bundles of energy that have not morphed into another system? I have an idea that ghosts are made up mostly from the energy of a human soul and a strong personality or sense of self. This might be why some ghosts speak to people. It might also explain why some ghosts appear dressed in clothing they used to wear when they were alive. People (and the writers of *The Matrix,* to be fair) talk about the subconscious image of your residual self. This is the mental image you keep in your mind, the version of yourself you see in dreams or imagine when you consider your ideal physical form. This could be why we see certain ghosts how they once were; spirits might unconsciously hold onto that internal vision of who they were and what they wore, therefore manifesting that image to the metaphysical. I know—there are lots of questions that follow that statement. That is why this is a hypothesis more than a theory, really.

There is another part to this. Paranormal groups talk about how certain energy sources drain or wan when spirits prepare to show themselves. Lights flash and batteries in various devices appear to go dead or weaken. The air can go cold or sometimes superheat to the point at which it becomes uncomfortable. Well, I have a plot thickener for that as well. The second law of thermodynamics asserts the existence of a quantity called the entropy of a system. That means that even when energy changes hands or the source breaks down, that energy does not dissipate;

it merely redistributes itself to a new place. So I hypothesize that maybe reactions with humans, electronics, and even the temperature in the air can allow the spirits to exchange or borrow energy from those sources, enabling them to reach a mutual thermodynamic equilibrium. Basically, the ghosts take the energy and manipulate it to their benefit. Once that energy is used, it can then find another system in which to adapt. Energy never goes away; it just switches sides when it is convenient. Maybe this is why some ghosts can seem less vibrant or coherent at times—because they have not been able to recapture and replenish their own energy, and even with a force of residual will, they cannot be the soul they were when they were alive or even freshly dead.

These are my points. A ghost—to me—is a strong soul with a stronger will, seeing itself as we see it and doing its best to borrow enough energy to continue. Some find a way to use external energy for its survival, thereby finding balance in the natural systems of the world. Others never develop that skill and slowly fade away, feeling their own natural energy ebb from constant use and never recovering when that energy does not return, joining the various systems of its surroundings. Sure, it is not perfect. In order for this to work, you have to believe the human will is powerful enough to manage malleable energy. In order for my scientific (hah) idea to mean anything, you have to concede that a personality is strong enough to control the power of a human soul even after death, unconsciously or otherwise. I cannot think that is too much to ask. We have seen the power of the human mind do incredible things: overcome pain, break down certain secrets of the universe, compete with computers, and so on. I do not see how this can be too far a reach into the potential of this fascinating flesh experiment called humanity.

Ghost hunters talk about EMF readings a lot. EMF stands for "electromagnetic field." Essentially these are fluctuations in the natural fields that surround us, because EMF readings are everywhere. Doubters are quick to point out that because of this reason, EMF readings are no good at differentiating between a spirit and, say, some sort of aberrant electrical wiring. However, using my intelligent energy hypothesis, this tends to back up what the paranormal establishment is saying, that EMF readings are indeed a solid way to find out if a ghost is nearby or possibly even trying to manifest and make contact. I grant you that sometimes EMF readings are just a proper way to establish whether or not you have a problem with your outlets and light fixtures. I mean, you can *feel* when faulty appliances and circuitry are spilling about; many people experience headaches, nausea, paranoia, and slight hallucinations. Sometimes a spade is a garden utensil. But sometimes a spade is the trump suit. Sometimes, what you are feeling very well may be what is actually going on.

But what do I know? I am a singer in a band, just trying desperately to get the masses to pay attention to my every move. I am prone to outbursts of profound berserker ramblings that fade into one-way lanes before overcorrecting to keep my Mopar mind on the road. I think all the time, and I cannot shut it off, often much to my own calamity. I am not complaining; I get more from thinking than I do from idling—you cannot race a parked car. So I tumble these fancies over and over in my brain like laundry in the dryer, flipping them about for coverage and praying my crotch is not soggy when I find myself wrapped inside them. I am the Buddha of babble—witness the vitriol and savor its profundity.

Skeptics are quick to call out anything as far-fetched as an idea like mine. Then again, cynical atheists are just as crackers as zealous religious nuts sometimes. They mock and fight and demand evidence—it always comes down to the evidence. Well, I quickly point out that the scientific society is *certain* of the existence of quarks, the particles that make up atoms. But they have never seen one. They are *certain* there are planets that can sustain life much like our own—an idea I happen to agree with. But they have never seen one. Before the Hadron Collider provided exasperatingly miniscule evidence of what scientists refers to as "dark matter"—the substance they say makes up space itself—they were *certain* of its existence. But they had never seen it, and the jury is still out on whether it is indeed dark matter. You have to remember: as smart and savvy as these people are, they are still *humans*. Until 1969 humans still considered homosexuality a mental illness, and hundreds of innocent people were persecuted because of it. To this day some people still believe homosexuality is something that can be "cured," which is disgusting. I defer to the scientific community on this one, because they have provided several examples of homosexuality in nearly every species on the planet. You are attracted to whomever you are attracted to; blame pheromones or Axe Body Spray. It is the way of the world. The point is that we can get it wrong, spectacularly at times. But God for-fucking-bid you try to get a stubborn prick biscuit to change his or her mind.

Speaking of the Almighty, just when I think I can get onboard with an idea like God, religion gets in the fucking way. I remember being on a press tour when all the violent protests broke out at the various embassies last year over the American movie *Innocence of Muslims* that purportedly made fun of the prophet Mohammed. People died, including an American ambassador and British soldiers. The Muslims of the world wonder why they are persecuted so much and so often. I give you exhibit A. I am not advocating this persecution—I am merely showing you why there might be such a penchant for global animosity. When any religion says it represents love and morality yet people who follow that religion lash out with constant ferocity when ideals do not line up with their own, that faith becomes synonymous with hypocrisy and hate. Christians can be just as bloody guilty. In my opinion if you say to the world that your way is the way to God and heaven and everlasting peace and other such rubbish, whether you are a Christian, Muslim, Jew, or Voodoo priest, you have a responsibility to humanity to try to make things better, not tear things apart. In fact, to "get religion" means "to resolve to mend one's errant ways." Maybe the religious should consider *getting* religion in lieu of just *being* one.

Let's get back to the reasonable side of the fence before I go off on another rabid tangent.

My hypothesis is something I am calling the "intelligent energy" idea. I am no mathematician, but I am certain that if I were, I could devise a wonderful formula for this idea. It would be something along the lines of "the soul (will added to energy) multiplied by infinity equals the spirit (surrounding energy fields divided by gravitational singularity to the Nth power)." I will give it a go in equation form: $S (W + E) \times \infty = $ ghosts. Not as elegant as I would have imagined from myself, but there it is. I am no Stephen Hawking, but I would say I lean toward a decent side of the fence. Then again, maybe not—I do say fuck a lot, and apparently using coarse language is a sign of a limited intelligence.

Well fuck you too, dick breath.

To sum up "intelligent energy," consider a ball of Silly Putty rolled onto a newspaper. Silly Putty, for those of you younger than I am (bastards), is a sort of Play Doh-like substance that is more rubber than clay. You can stretch it out, bounce it like a ball, chew it up if you are *truly* disgusting, or do what is also suggested on the box it comes in—use it to make transfers from pictures in newspapers. The ink adheres to the Silly Putty, giving you a mirror image transfer that you can then pull and manipulate into different shapes and macabre cartoons. It can be a lot of fun—well, at least for a generation who did not grow up with *Assassin's Creed 3*.

My idea of "intelligent energy" has that same kind of slant to it. Essentially the soul is the newspaper and the energy is the Silly Putty. I believe a strong enough will—or soul—can impress itself onto outside energy, enabling it to carry on in a state sort of like a loop in this world. Because that energy cannot be destroyed, the energy of the soul joins that energy and becomes something completely different, what we refer to as a ghost. In that way the intelligence of that spirit carries on without the body to fuel it, seeing as it can adhere itself to as much energy as it can get its "hands" on. Yes, I know—sounds a bit weird, right? But if you take into consideration the lower system in the body—the intestines, colon and such—which can continue to run itself even when disconnected from the brain and the central nervous system, something like "intelligent energy" existing in nature does not seem like such a far-fetched idea. Maybe I am right and maybe I am wrong; like I said before, it is only an interesting concept. I have done no experiments to prove these things—this is all patchy guesswork on my end.

I think my own brain loves to get me in trouble sometimes, sort of a double agent sabotage attempt. The things that seem to make complete sense to me at the time tend to make other people openly stare at the sad man with a beard like a leprechaun. Maybe I can get away with it if I just plead "ginger" sometimes. I really enjoy the idea that redheads like me (sort of) are regarded as soulless weirdoes. So I use this to my advantage a lot—especially in Britain. If I am feeling a bit apathetic that day, I tell people my ginger is acting up, and they seem to buy that. But now that I think about that a little too much, I am wondering . . . are there any redheaded ghosts? Well, according to some, gingers have no soul. So how could a soulless ginger leave behind a spirit? This might require more research. It could be that gingers do not die—we just melt and reconstitute as a different ginger baby. Maybe we absorb the energy around us to fill the deep chasm where we should feel things like . . . feelings. OOH! What if redheads eat ghosts? What a wonderful idea! Could you imagine, if you were dealing with a poltergeist and an exorcism did not work, sending in a ginger that is really peckish? Their mouth would elongate like the "Come to Daddy" video by Aphex Twin, and they would just suck any spirits into the heart of their redheadedness, powering its gingery ways for a few more days.

I apologize to my ruddy brothers and sisters for perpetuating the stereotype that we are soulless bastards. I look forward to all of your angrily written letters and of course the verbal confrontations at our next secret meeting. Now, moving on . . .

Let's talk about heaven for a while. Now, different religions have different ideas of what heaven would be or look like. The Christian version has all the trappings of cloudy condominiums guarded by blokes with wings. Muslims have honey and an inordinate amount of virgins. Jews, I believe, have lots of cake and no guilt from their mothers—but I am of course guessing. You would think Jewish heaven would essentially be a bigger chunk of Christian heaven, seeing as the front half of the Bible, the Old Testament, is a version of the Torah that has been revised and rewritten countless times by multiple people. So maybe Heaven is a Christian time-share and the Jews are the landlords. That is, if you believe in the idea of heaven anyway. Where the hell would it be? Would it be up in the rings of Saturn? Or would it be some sort of sideways dimension? Or is heaven a sort of gossamer reality where souls can shift in and out, back onto our side of that fence?

That looks very pretty on a computer screen, but it means fuck all in the real world. Hence all my grammatical babble. The more I wear this itchy skin suit, the more I realize that most humans can talk huge amounts of beautifully sounding bullshit, disguised as expounding on philosophical pontifications. Verbiage is a great way of throwing sawdust on the vomit that so-called intellects secrete in their wake, leaving us stranded on a pub crawl on a dead Saturday. As far as I can make out, the only difference between a scholar and a snake oil salesman is the degree to which they try to sway you to their way of thinking. Be that as it may, I like to subscribe to waxings like those that history has given us over time, but that does not mean I am the DH for either team. So I have made up my own mind, but as legendary New York Yankees manager Casey Stengel pointed out, "I made it up both ways."

Jumping back on the more thrilling side of the wall, tales of spirits walking among us have been prevalent since print tied remote ends of countries together. Abraham Lincoln, my absolute favorite president, is said to stroll the halls of the White House and visit guests staying in the bedroom that bears his name. Ulysses S. Grant is supposedly "seen" in the lobby of the Willard Hotel in Washington D.C., lounging in his favorite chair and enjoying one of his trademark cigars; people say you can still smell the cigar smoke linger even after he has moved on. On the topic of hotels, the Roosevelt in Los Angeles apparently has several instances of paranormal activity, including but not limited to visits in various rooms from a female specter resembling Marilyn Monroe and the haunting sounds of invisible gala soirees in the spacious ballroom. It sort of begs the question: is it the place that attracts these phantom imprints or is it the "will" of the wraith itself, going where it chooses to create a veritable cycle, like a DVD menu in which no one hits the play button?

Alcatraz Prison in San Francisco has a very popular ghost tour, where they guide you through the mazes that made up that citadel of crime for years. That would be something I would love to do sometime. Your chances are 50/50 either way of seeing something or seeing nothing, but imagine getting away from the tour and looking around without a chaperone. Ooh! That would be some sphincter-tightening shit—wandering around almost exclusively in a rundown old jailhouse, waiting for something to happen. I would be in a fit of heavens. Then again, what are the odds that if there *were* some residual haunts hanging about, they would keep their hands to themselves? Could you imagine suddenly being assaulted by thieves and murderers from beyond the modern veil of reality? They sure as fuck would be pissed off and ready to shank a motherfucker in the face. Of course, their shanks would probably pass right through you, but my experience has taught me that if the souls of the dearly departed want to move you, they can and will. I will tell you more about that later, but trust me—it will give you pause if you start some shit with Casper the Gnarly Ghost.

Speaking of strange happenings in jails, when I was a teenager I spent a lot of my summer nights in a town called Indianola, Iowa, which is about fifteen minutes from Des Moines. It is where most of my close cousins grew up, so, hanging out there, I made a lot of friends. It is not a big town; you can get from one

end to the other in about ten minutes, and that is being gener-
ous. The center of town was a one-block-by-one-block concoc-
tion of one-story buildings and shops that were dominated by
the courthouse/jail right in the middle of it all. We called it the
Square, and even though the cop shop was there, that was where
we all hung out, either cruising in a constant combo of left turns
or parking and sitting on car trunks. In another example of not
really giving a flat shit whether or not the police seemed to be
nearby, we also either got high or drunk or both, depending on
what was what from who and where. I spent a lot of nights, head
spinning and laughing uncontrollably, sitting with my friends on
the Square. This was where I discovered, much to my chagrin,
that you could be arrested for pretending to be a blind person.
Then again, maybe it was more about the fact that I was mocking
with an attitude the policeman who tried to make us disperse,
calling us a "gang." I think you can understand by now that I
have no time for small-minded people with silly hang-ups.

Anyway, there was a legend in Indianola about one of the jailhouse windows. It was said that long ago a man was murdered
in one of the cells with his face pushed up against the window,
screaming in agony and fighting to get the window open, maybe
to get help or get out. The story goes that because he met his end
in such a violent way, that window was impressed with the scene
and the spirit of the doomed man. If I am quoting this right, "to
this day, at the right time day or night, you could see the man
with his face plastered to the glass, silently trying to fight off his
unseen assailant." As local legends go, you have to admit that is a
pretty decent juicy one. It has action, drama, gore, and a hint of
unnerving imagery. I have no idea if it is true or not, but I can
tell you on good authority that my friends and I stared at every
window on that building nearly every night for a whole summer

trying to get a glimpse of this crazy ghostly attack. Sure, we were high and drunk. But what the hell else are you going to do on a Friday during the summer in a town where the dominant landmarks are fucking cornfields? I can safely say I never saw anything happen in the jailhouse window . . . although I did witness a girl in a skirt pick up a beer can without using her hands. You all have sufficiently dirty minds—you do the math.

Then one night something happened to me while I was hanging out in Indianola.

Surrounding this little town were suburbs, the aforementioned cornfields, and hundreds of gravel roads that seemingly led to the edges of nowhere. When we were not camped out on the Square getting our jollies on, we were out in the darkened country speeding into the pitch black, doing things like handstands in truck beds and playing Mailbox Baseball, which is exactly what it sounds like. If I had any misconceptions about how crazy certain people in Des Moines were, the kids I hung out with in Indianola made them all look like fucking amateurs. People fought and fucked freely, sometimes all at once. It was the spirit of the caged animal trying desperately to feel the sting of freedom on its dry and cracking lips. You can cover a lot of ground with complete abandon—you just need the right set of car keys. Our lives would have given Grant Wood an all-American Gothic hard-on, complete with pitchforks and dour sex in parking lots.

One very eventful night my friends and I were out amongst the livestock and misty rural terrain, getting fucked up and thereby fucking up everything around us. We had pulled up just off of a crazy abandoned road fairly removed from 65–69, which was the main interstate artery that ran through the town. A few pathetic streetlights spilled a pinch of illumination around us, giving our maladjusted eyes views of the corn, the trees, the road, and each other. We had pulled off slightly, because to pull all the way over would have meant driving into a drainage ditch. The moon was soft and subliminal. We all sat around our parked cars, drinking beer and Schnapps and whatever else. Thankfully it was not a Scotchgard night: I tended to go mental when I huffed that shit. For a full week I was convinced I could see the future after a nightmare of an evening spent inhaling that bastard stuff. But that is another story for another book. Back to the action . . .

I was taking a swig from a whiskey bottle when I saw the black shape in the corn.

I damn near spit it out—I had not heard any movement or seen any car lights. As far as I was concerned we were the only people out there. Then, before I could bring it to anyone else's attention, one of my friends saw it as well. It looked like a naked man, a living silhouette blending in with the cornstalks yet sticking out like a sore throbbing thumb. It was perhaps ten yards away from us, but we saw it clear as day. Then we blinked and it was gone. It freaked us out so bad that we had to laugh. Someone thought it was some kind of undercover cop. That little tidbit made us laugh even fucking harder. The laughter died abruptly, however, when we saw the same black shape on the road behind us.

We scrambled into our cars and trucks, people screaming and yelling. The thing was getting closer. I threw myself into one of the truck beds and demanded the driver hit the fucking gas pedal and get us the hell out of there. As bad luck would have it, the truck I had escaped to ended up being the last vehicle in our terrified convoy. So for all intents and purposes, I was face to fucking face with this thing. It chased us for a while, keeping up even as we ramped up the speeds. I did not know it, but I found myself screaming at it—"FUCK YOU! LEAVE US ALONE!" The scene had triggered something in my head, taking me back to that night in Cold House. I was a ten-year-old kid again, trying to get my leg unstuck from rotting wood and cursing myself for having this stupid idea in the first place. Thankfully my buddy was steady on the wheel, and as we swung our ass ends out onto the pavement of the interstate, the black shape vanished without a trace.

When we got back to the Square, it was my childhood all over again: some of us wanted to talk about it, and others refused to say anything. I was one of those silent few. I was shaking like a dog shitting cockle burrs. I wanted to go home and hide under my bed. I never wanted to hear another thing about ghosts and shapes and evil ever again. I sat quietly, even when a sort of "ghost posse" formed in the wake of those events and several people from the Square went off to try to find the thing again, including people who were not there the first time. For me, I had seen enough. I crashed at a friend's house, and the next morning I went back to Des Moines. It was a while before I made it back to the Square in Indianola again. By then people were tired of talking about the Thing in the Corn, as they called it. They were back to Wake & Bakes and beer bongs, and this put me back at ease. Since that day, though, I have always been on guard. I never truly relax. I am always waiting, ready for that darkness to come running out of the corn for me.

Do I unconsciously draw this nonsense to me? Or is this stuff naturally attracted to me? After everything I have seen, I am not so sure. Honestly I am inclined to look at myself as some freaky conduit. Between Cold House and the Kids on the Circle, which we will get to soon enough, the argument can be made that there is something about me that stirs the vibrations in all kinds of crazy shit. But I have refused to give in to anything in me that wants to straight split and run away. I carry on with the avenues of life. Whether you believe me or not is irrelevant; what matters is that I have not and will not let these things control how I spend my time, love my people, or live my life. This is the hand I have been dealt. I hope you are ready to go all in, because I could double down at any moment. Never bet on the flop or the river; set your lot on the cards in front of you. The more I look at things on a level plain, the more those simple things that matter the most carry on being your foundation. My backstory may be set, but I will never shit-can the plot just because it begins to thicken.

I say this not to brag on myself, but maybe these strong personalities are attracted to other strong personalities. Anyone who knows me is thoroughly aware that I am a boisterous blowhard with a propensity for cracking off at the mouth and laughing out loud even when it is inappropriate. In other words, I bow my head for the National Anthem but I am not afraid to tell a dirty joke at a funeral. The funny thing is electricity and magnetism have the same properties—we will talk more about that in another chapter. But assume for a second there is a magnetic attraction between two sets of energy. Who is to say one large bundle of energy cannot become attracted to another and follow it to where it resides? Would that explain something like spirits clinging to a living person and taking up in each home the living person chooses to live? Maybe. Then again, maybe I am mad as a hatter and I have no muzzle for the crazy shit that comes out of my mouth. Only time will tell.

So to sum up this chapter, between reality and madness lies the world we all call home. I have a foot in both of those pies, and no matter how hectic it gets in here, my reason keeps me swinging. All I need is a minute or two to work it all out. If I can get my head around it, I will find a way to understand it, even if it does not make sense to everyone else right away—or ever for that matter. It is like my own personal Kobayashi Maru and I am James Tiberius Kirk, cheating my way to a way out. Seeing as the captain and I are both from Iowa, I think that parallel will work just fine. That is because as long as there is hope, life will always go on. It could be the darkest side of hell you have ever witnessed—if you hang on long enough to carry on, you will. With these strange equations and unsettling stories both creating surplus in my head, I have a way to broker a modest ceasefire between my fear and my understanding. It gives me sure footing when I walk out into those cold nights, when something in the air threatens to wreak a bit of havoc on your good vibes. Bring it on—I have enough experience to know how to handle it.

In the dark we all experience that same brief sense of panic before sleep takes us into its arms. There is something underneath our skin where the ancient bits of our minds still have purchase that always keeps a watchful eye when we are alone and vulnerable. It could be that is the bit that still has the eyes for this sort of phenomena. Call it what you want—fight or flight, predation sensory, sixth sense, paranoia—it is all the same thing at the end of the day: a hyperactive itch that warns us if there is trouble brewing in our general area. This could be one of the faculties that keeps us on our toes and wary when it comes to things like spirits and poltergeists. It also could be the very perception that confuses our minds and lets us see something that might not be there. However this slice of our conscious and unconscious mind works, its strange ways will keep us searching through the mysteries of this world—and the next. Maybe we will never know if these things are real or not. But the human mind will continue its quest for answers long after the questions become small enough to wrap our heads around.

So much for pathos . . .

FOSTER MANOR

ONE NIGHT IN 2005 my son Griffin called me into his room in the old house we were living in at the time. He had just turned three, but he was still very adamant that when I was home, he wanted me to stay in his room with him. I knew he would eventually have to grow out of this, so one night I asked him why he wanted me to sleep in his room with him all the time. He said, very solemnly, "Well, because when you are in here, the Shadow Man stops keeping me awake."

That sentence gives me goose pimples to this day.

Over ten years ago I did not know any of this was going to happen. All I knew was that I had a son on the way and I had to find a family home that was *also* a decent investment for my hard-earned money; all I had done so far was wipe my ass on rent for a two-bedroom apartment in a renovated split-level that sat between the mayor of Des Moines' house and a certified crack den. I know what you are thinking: "But Corey, that sounds like the perfect mix of hearth and home to affix said family to for all eternity!" May I remind you that, one, no one talks like that, and two, even if they did, that still would not make that vile line of drivel true.

I wanted to buy a house, but not just any house. I wanted a fucking manor house. I wanted something that would give Bruce Wayne a giant envy boner on a bitterly cold Christmas night. I wanted a construct of abnormal proportions that would cause those who beheld it to freeze in their tracks and wonder who lived there. I wanted a compound of such amazing stature that I could walk outside and feel like a Bond villain on his day off, stroking some sort of white cat and trying in vain to keep my crappy monocle in my eye, even though I really did not need it. When I was younger I had always had a fantasy about living in a deconsecrated church like a superhero. Now that I was older, my

tastes had become more advanced and realistic; I knew super-
heroes did not have to live in abandoned churches. I just needed
a house that *looked* like a superhero lived there.

So we scoured the real estate ads like madmen on a mission.
Nothing seemed to fit my "reasonable" criteria, but I was unde-
terred. Meanwhile the bridge near the apartment I was living in
had been blown to bits for reconstruction. Unfortunately, I forgot all about the planned blasting, and it knocked the shit out of
the living room, throwing Spiderman wall mounts and family
pictures every which way. That was the nail in the coffin lid for
me. But my resolve was beginning to fade—at one point I
thought we would never find the right house and we would have
to settle for less. After a seemingly fruitless search, however, a
listing caught my eye that was too good to be true, both for the
asking price and the neighborhood in which it was ensconced.

There is a district in Des Moines known as South of Grand.
For decades this suburb was the seat of wealth and the well-to-
do in town. All my life, friends of mine have driven through that
neighborhood, gazing on the illustrious houses and beautifully
manicured yards, and they would pontificate about owning one
of these mansions, living a life of luxury and opulence. Most of
the time they were high as shit and had Doritos cheese dust on
their fingers and pants, but you could see in their eyes this was a
real hope, a true dream that if they ever got the chance to realize
it, they would be in hog heaven. I am not ashamed to say I was
one of those dreamers. The houses in that burg are wondrous little capsules of history. You can imagine my excitement when I
found myself in the mix to own a house in that very area.

It was a three-story, four-bedroom, three-and-one-half bathroom brick colonial house on Foster Drive, built in 1905 and
smack dab where all the elitist heads of commerce used to live

throughout Des Moines' years in industry. It also had a basement, a two-car garage, a pool, a hot tub, and a nice big yard with
a rolling hill. It fulfilled two separate ideals for me: it was South
of Grand and it seemed like a perfect place to raise a son. It was
listed for what they refer to as a song, and even though the
amenities were not what you would call "modern" (it had last
been remodeled in the 1980s), it was the obvious choice for me
to expend a good amount of my portion of the coin of the realm.
A one-hundred-year-old mansion in the most prestigious neighborhood in town? Where the fuck do I sign? I bid on it, we got
it, and we moved in shortly before Griffin was born.

Trouble kicked up dust before we had even moved a scrap of
furniture. A very nice lady from the *Des Moines Register* (our local paper) called me to do a "little interview for the Real Estate
section." I obliged and babbled for a few minutes. She thanked
me for my time and hung up the phone. Two days later the front
page of the newspaper read, "Slipknot Singer Buys House in Historical District." It went on to show a photo of the house and
gave the fucking address. It also quoted me as saying, "Besides
the blood sacrifices on Thursdays, it would be a relatively quiet
life in the neighborhood," which is really the way to cultivate
new friendships in an area full of people who most certainly will
be scared to death of the big bad rock star moving in. I was livid.
I called the newspaper, and the nice lady I had done the interview with said that her editor had decided to make it a front-
page story. No one considered the fact that I would have to deal
with hundreds of fans just stopping by to say hello or bug me for
an autograph, which they did. I was in the driveway one day
when the same car full of drunken idiots drove by ten times
screaming, "SLIPKNOT! YEAH!" My neighbors were less than
enthused.

But that did not stop me from thoroughly loving the place. The house was wonderful. The basement was finished, with an old-time brass bar. The first floor consisted of a mudroom walkway, which opened to the dining room; kitchen just off of the dining room and the main hall; the living room to your left; and off of that was the solarium, an enclosed and heated patio added fifty years after the house was originally built. The second floor had the four bedrooms, of which the master bedroom had a door that opened to a sort of veranda on top of the solarium. The third floor was a finished attic, replete with a bathroom of its own. In fact, all the floors had bathrooms. It seems since 1905 people have always needed easy access to a place to leave a shit. The attic gnawed at me. I never felt comfortable there. It was always either completely cold or horrendously hot. I chalked it up to a one-hundred-year-old house and its many idiosyncrasies.

I had not lived there very long before a presence made it frustratingly clear we were roommates, not out-and-out owners.

I was putting dishes away in the kitchen. The sun was pouring through the windows, and I had a good CD in the old boom box. You guys remember what a boom box is, right? A boom box is a ghetto blaster. Fuck's sake, you have no idea what a ghetto blaster is either? A ghetto blaster was the original thing you played music on, when music came on things like cassette tapes and CDs as opposed to megabytes and downloads. You played these ancient bits of entertainment on a CD player of some sort, not a computer. These CD players—and I might just blow your mind on this one—were either components for a home stereo system or portable radios that *also* had the ability to play CDs. The latter is what is known as a boom box or ghetto blaster. That is what was in my kitchen that day playing music. If you feel like doing some research on these now-defunct relics of industry, Google "stuff before you were born." Or better yet, Google "modes of playing music back when music was worth listening to." An even better search would be "how you listened to music when there was no possible way to fucking steal it and spread it to the rest of your thieving dick-stain friends."

Sorry—I am a bitter old man who does not care about your feelings. Suck it.

As I was saying, I was putting stuff away in the kitchen. Mind you, at the time, I was not one for domesticity. I was usually the one who would pull up a bucket of chicken and veg on the couch for a month or seven. But I was excited—I had never had my own home before. Yes, I had my own apartment and had lived on my own for a long time. I had even spent a long time living on the streets. But I had never been a homeowner. I never even thought that would be an option. Here I was, putting dishes away in a house that had my name on it. This was my house. This was my castle. I felt great. That feeling diminished slightly when a vase was shoved off a counter not five feet away from where I was standing. That sort of thing tends to knock the sugar off of your doughnut. It scared the everlasting out of me. My heart crawled back into my chest after plummeting into my asshole temporarily. I cleaned up the shattered glass and went back to what I was doing, with a watchful eye for something else to happen.

I settled into a nice routine of balancing growing pains with the self-fulfilling prophecy of home ownership. South of Grand is a stone's throw away from the urbane of the urban city, but it was set against an expanse of forest that stretched clear back past where the last bit of property ended. As a result of this, packs of crazy deer ran through the front yard all the fucking time. It became a bizarre version of *Logan's Run* whenever it was time to put the trash out on the curb. I remember someone running the canisters down to the street, turning around slowly, and finding him or herself surrounded by eight or nine of these wild cocksuckers. It was apparently chilly that night, because these deer were snorting out foggy breath through their flaring nostrils in an intimidating manner. There was a tense moment when a buck with huge antlers bent his head like he would lash out, but a car happened to drive by and they split up, running into the night like a bunch of four-legged burglars looking for another score. Since then, I do not fuck around with wildlife—I just keep my bat close by.

The paranormal action stayed mundane for some time—that is, if you can call "unseen hands pushing heavy crystal vessels off of high places" mundane in the first place. What is more, it was random—nothing would happen for a few days, and then doors would slam off and on for twenty-four hours. Friends would come over for dinner only to have their hair pulled later while sitting and talking. I would hear running up and down the stairs at all hours night and day. Then it would stop . . . nothing. The lapse would last long enough that I would forget about these things, only for the strangeness to return tenfold.

For the most part, however, the activity seemed to be consigned to the third floor. I would hear pacing, slow and steady, treading the floors of the attic above. But the real testimony came from the people who stayed on that third floor. Things were just very wrong on that level of the house. Whether they were just staying overnight or they were living in the attic for an extended period of time, guests would hear voices in the early hours when no one else was awake. They would see out of the corner of their eyes dark shapes moving in the peripheral spaces. Worse yet, they were being physically assaulted in their sleep. One friend woke up with long, thin welts up and down her legs. It looked like someone had taken a pen or a pencil, heated it up, and smacked the shit out of the skin. Another friend discovered welts in the shapes of strange letters and writing. One of the other troubling factors was that everyone who slept on the third floor looked pale and drawn, white as a sheet and unrested. They all seemed like they had a vitamin or iron deficiency, floating slowly through the house like ghosts themselves. I was horrified—what in the sheer, silky fuck was going on up in that damn room?

To be fair, my attention was in other places. Griffin was a handful as a baby, and I spent most of my time feeding him, singing to him so he would take a nap, or keeping him from crawling off a ledge once he became mobile. Remember, I was in and out of town on tour a lot—in fact, I had to leave for the first Stone Sour tour only ten days after he was born. So I was with him every chance I could get. I would get up with him for his nightly feedings, putting on a movie downstairs and placing my son on a pillow so I could prop him on my lap and give him his bottle. I cannot tell you how many times I let that poor kid watch *Evil Dead 2: Dead by Dawn* while I fell asleep with a bottle in his mouth. That could be one of the reasons he is so crazy today, so maybe it was a good thing. I was trying to be a good dad, or what I thought constituted being a good dad, seeing as I had no practice of my own and no basis for comparison because I had no father growing up. Because of that, my son and I developed a bond that has thankfully lasted to this day. He is My Boy, and he makes me proud.

It was while I was with my son as a tiny little guy that my first physical confrontation happened with the shadowy residents of the Foster Manor. Until that point I had listened to the descriptions from the people hanging out on the third floor with fascination—I had never experienced anything like that. I did not doubt them—I mean, the evidence was right there on their bodies, for fuck's sake—I just had nothing to identify with from that side of the coin. As far as I was concerned, as long as Griff was okay, I was minding my own business. I gave little thought to these issues as I watched my son in the mornings, feeding him and making sure he stayed out of dangerous chemicals while occasionally singing him to sleep in his swing.

One morning I was carrying him down the stairs to make him a bottle. It was early—the sun is not your friend after four hours of sleep. But as a dad, your job in the early years is really just the survival of your kin. So fuck sleep—grab the moo juice. I figured I would get him settled and put on some TV, relax, maybe even nap while he napped. It seemed like such a simple plan. I was spacing out, heading down the stairs, focused on getting to the kitchen, when I was pushed from behind. I felt it right in the middle of my back. I was pushed so hard, my chest shoved straight out. It surprised me with its force. I found myself falling down the stairs with my son in my arms. The only thing I could do was twist my body in midair so I landed on my back with him on my chest. It knocked the wind out of me, and I bounced my head on the hardwood floor. My boy started screaming instantly. I lifted my eyes up to where I had just been, and of course, as always, there was not a soul in sight.

Now I was fucking pissed. I was on fire—a pissed off German Irish bastard who was ready to break shit with a cricket bat in order to protect his kid from danger, even if that meant going crazy and doing something stupid. I could feel my teeth gritting and my knuckles popping. My jaw hurt from flexing and my eyes were dry from staring down molecules because there was nothing else around for me to mean mug. By Grape Soda, I was dying for some action! I needed to bypass caveman mode and go right to Machiavellian evil. Something had threatened the brood, and I wanted to torture it until it felt as helpless as I did at that moment, trying to calm down a little boy who had just flown through the air and not of his own volition. I wanted war like a monger lusts for power, and I set out to find it on my own.

So one night when the boy was at his grandmother's house, I got drunk and went into the attic to challenge the invisible slits to a fight.

I know: this was a colossal waste of time and effort. But this was 2003, which was during what I call my Dark Period. So my idea of fixing a problem in those days was to chug whiskey and smash it to bits with a hammer, only to wake up much later with a headache and a much bigger problem. But no matter—it made sense to me, so it made sense, full stop. I charged drunkenly up the stairs and started yelling at fuck all. "Come on, ya cocksuckers! I am ready for you now! Let's see how fucking tough you are when a guy is looking! And when he is not holding a fucking toddler!" That was pretty much the routine for a couple hours before I got bored and wandered back down the stairs to eat cold fried chicken. I can feel how impressed you are by that very male display of domination. I also cook bacon without wearing a shirt. Fuck the hot grease—I feel nothing but manly hunger! When no one is looking, however, I do apply a nice salve to the tiny burns. That shit feels like microscopic knife wounds.

I know what you are thinking, so I will answer your question: no, nothing happened that night. I did spill my drink all over the place, thus spending an entire afternoon trying to get the stain out. All hail the mighty warrior . . . dude guy. So much for alcohol and bravado; in this instance pathos goes out the window with subtlety and wisdom. But when something happens to me and mine, I freak out like a maniac. You do not poke the fucking bear. The Shadow Man is lucky I could not get my hands around his supposedly scrawny neck. I would have wrung him out like an old dishrag full of suds and evil. My anger eventually dissipated, and I got back to doing constructive things like rolling down the hill in the front yard with Griffin clinging to my chest and laughing his ass off. But I still got some sand in the craw about that whole situation. What is the statute of limitations on being fucking pissed at a ghost? I might have to do some research in the Library of Congress on that one.

It was not all bad in the Foster Manor. Even though I was having difficulties in my relationship at the time, there were some good times as well. I watched my boy swim in our hot tub when he was still very small, his arms clad in Pool Buddies, which are essentially inflatable cuffs for your upper arms so you can float. He absolutely loved it. The only problem was that he loved it *so* much that he only ever wanted to swim in the hot tub. Even when he got older, all he wanted to do was jump in and out of the jacuzzi. There sat a massive pool for him to swim back and forth in, but he would not have it. He just liked doing ridiculous cannonballs into the hot tub. It was not until much later that we were able to coax him into "the big-boy pool." Now the kid is a damn fish; it does not matter what time of year it is, all he wants to do is get in the pool. Even when I let him get in when it is a bit cold and his lips turn purple and blue, he gets very upset when my wife or I insist on his departure into the warmth of the house. I do *not* know where he gets his stubbornness from sometimes . . .

You! Yeah . . . YOU. Shut your inner mouth.

There were some good grown-up times as well. I can remember a fairly inebriating evening of cocktails and shenanigans that was going swimmingly—a party for the professionals, if you will.

Unfortunately there is a giant lapse in my memory around this point, but I do recall coming around in my kitchen, standing at the sink, and eating the smallest BBQ sandwich I had ever seen with no pants on. I do not know where my pants went. I do not know where the sandwich came from. All I know is it was very cold in my kitchen and pants would have been a good thing—especially with all the partygoers saying goodbye and staring rather rudely. But as far as I was concerned, my house plus my kitchen equaled my prerogative. There were nights of wonderful games like Trivial Pursuit and Scene It. One night some friends and I learned how to play Texas Hold 'Em, and I got cleaned the fuck out by those same prick-like friends. At least they left me with a shirt I could wear. Things would seem normal for long periods. I would only hear fleeting things about other experiences up on the third floor.

Also the damage perpetrated in this house was not always consigned to the spiritual wrecking crew. There was a night when the kids were at Grandma's house and we had some friends over for a few tee many martoonis. Around four in the morning I was trying in vain to get those friends to simply crash at the house; it was clear they were too inebriated to drive themselves home. After a round of arguments and a sneaky exit, these stalwart friends ended up driving backward through my front yard and colliding dangerously with a telephone pole. Another foot to the right and they would have taken out my neighbor's mailbox. On a different occasion someone ran around my house during a Halloween party, spitting beer all over my walls. It may have been years ago, but if I find the son of a bitch who did it, I just may dig a pit and toss his or her body in with a nice little lye bath for good measure. It is probably the same motherfucker who stole one of my black Gibson Les Paul customs I had stashed in the basement so no one would see them. God, I hate thieves as much as I hate cold coffee sometimes.

One day Griffin's grandmother was taking the trash down to the corner so it could be collected the next morning. As she was depositing the receptacles at the curb, a big white van pulled up full of Japanese tourists with cameras. They climbed out of the vehicle and immediately started taking pictures of her and the house. Needless to say, she was a little perturbed and asked what the hell was going on. They explained to her that they had been sold a "Map of Slipknot" at the airport, so they had rented a van to take them around to snap souvenir pictures. Griffin's grandmother waved them off, and I tried to warn the other band members that weirdness was coming their way in the form of a van full of tourists.

Oh and by the way, just so I can put to rest some scuttlebutt that has been spread across the landscapes of Facebook, Twitter, and even the desolate frozen wasteland that is still Myspace: I HAVE NEVER DONE DRUGS WITH ANY PERSON IN ANY OF THE BATHROOMS IN ANY OF THE HOUSES THAT I HAVE OWNED, LIVED IN, OR OTHERWISE. I do not know where this shitty sordid rumor started, but apparently there are a virtual *host* of assholes in Des Moines and other places that claim to have done all kinds of chemicals with yours truly while sequestered in one of my commodes. I have thrown many a party, even one that included wild livestock and a crash helmet (that was one hell of a birthday, I will say), but I have never imbibed or offered any illegal controlled substances with or to any people since 1989. The only thing other than alcohol I have ever partaken in was weed and mushrooms, and both of those were in Holland and Los Angeles. So all you mother fuckers who keep passing that brag around like a blow-up doll at a frat squat can just let it go because it is absolutely not true. However, there *were* two different times when cocaine was offered to me in a bathroom, but both those times were in Los Angeles as well. Ironically, both of those times involved well-known actors; one was at the old Viper Room (while said actor was trying to chat up a Puerto Rican boy in an attempt to get him to come home with him) and the other was deep inside our old friend from a few chapters ago, the Mansion. So just to sum up: I have never done any drugs in any of the bathrooms located in any of my old or current houses with any individual, alive or dead, but I myself was offered drugs in a couple bathrooms by B-List movie stars amid strange goings-on and whatnot. I hope this clears up any confusion in that land of facts and truth, the Internet.

As you may have read in my previous book and as I have said in interviews, it was right around Griffin's first birthday when I, quote unquote, "started to get my shit together." What followed was a three-year period when I did not touch a drop of alcohol and I started to get my focus back on work, family, and responsibility. That is hard shit for someone who has made a bloody mess of a lot of things, but you just have to keep slogging at it until it gets a bit more tolerable. So during this time frame I had that first conversation with Griffin about the Shadow Man. This was a very new development; up until that point there were really just the odd brushes with invisible antagonists. If anything, every once in a while you would see something quick and abrupt in the corner of your eye. But when a father hears his son describe "a man in the corner who keeps me awake," you bet your fat ass I take it seriously.

Some of you might be saying, "Well, he was three or four at the time, and kids have amazingly vivid imaginations, right?" Trust me, the thought crossed my mind. But studies have also shown that as children develop early on, they have a sort of extra perception for certain things. I am not talking about ESP; I am talking about being able to see things in a way that adults cannot after a while. Maybe it is because, as we get older, our minds fill with what is supposed to be real. Maybe we lose it because most people are taught that things like that do not exist and, because everyone else thinks that, your mind refuses to see them anymore. It is a possibility—God and Adam know stranger things have happened.

I also had to take into consideration that he might have wanted me to sleep in his room with him because I was on the road a lot and my times at home with him were precious and few. So there was the guilt-trip side to the story. But my son at that age really had no manipulative bones in his body. Plus, I remember the look on his face: he really saw this thing. He said the Shadow Man would stand in the corner looking at him, and every once in a while he would walk toward the bed and lean in at him. Griff would bury his face in the covers until the Shadow Man disappeared. But he always came back. So I took to sleeping in his room with him every once in a while, just to keep the Shadow Man at bay as much as I could.

One night I was in Griff's room, and my son was fast asleep. I was kind of in and out of consciousness—you know that feeling when you are just on the cusp of passing out? It can be a fertile ground for dreams and the like. So my eyelids were heavy, and I found myself slowly but surely nodding off. That was when I finally got my first glimpse of the Shadow Man with my own eyes. At first I was not truly convinced I was seeing things clearly. There was a moment when I thought it was part of my dream. Then I thought, "Well why would I dream about this spot in Griff's bedroom?" Once I woke up fully and realized he was still there, I found I could not move. He stood in the corner, exactly as the boy had said, just staring at us. His face was pale, and he never blinked. Finally he made as if to walk toward the bed. I suddenly shot bolt upright, not sure what the hell I was going to do against a flipping ghost but damn sure I was not going to let him fuck with my son again. But it turned out it did not matter because as soon as I moved, he vanished. I watched it happen. It was incredibly fascinating and terribly unsettling all at the same time. We were only in that house for another year, but the Shadow Man never came back, even when I was gone at work.

Things died down for a bit. If there was anything going on, nobody really noticed. Griff's mother and I were beginning to separate, so it is easy to say that my attention was otherwise elsewhere. By the middle of 2006 we were no longer together, and neither of us was living in Foster Manor. It seems so strange to call it that now. It was just an old house on an old side of town that just so happened to come with extra residents. But to me it represented less the start of a new life and more the beginning of the life I lead now. It was a foray into adulthood by a "man" who should have started much earlier than he allowed himself. Had I done that, I am sure things would have turned out much the same. But having said that, I still have no regrets. I am exactly where I am meant to be in my life. Griff's mom and I have both met fantastic people whom we married, and between the two couples we do our best to raise Griffin to be a good, intelligent, and creative boy, which he definitely is today.

A crazy side note: after I sold the house to a nice doctor and his wife, a storm knocked down one of the big trees in the yard and it smashed into Foster Manor! I could not believe it—a friend of mine told me about it. I did not want to imagine anything happening to that one-hundred-seven-year-old house; I mean, the thing had survived *two* great floods in Des Moines *and* a barrage of looting that happened in 1992. Now a massive tree was threatening to destroy this beautiful house. Soon after, thankfully, the owners began putting things back together. I happened to drive by the other day, and nothing looked too broken down or demolished. So at least that little corner in the National Historical Index is still there and will continue to be for another hundred years or more.

I would be remiss if I did not tell you the final tale of Foster Manor, which happened just before I sold the house. It spooked me so bad that I never went back—I got all my stuff out as quickly as possible and fled, leaving a few things in my wake that I can only hope the new owners put to good use. Anyway, it caught me off guard and thrust me back to everything that had happened there. The wounds, the smashed glass, the assault, the Shadow Man—all of these things came flooding back into my memory, and beautiful house or not, there was no fucking way I was going to climb the steps to that place ever again. Better grab a piss now, because I do not plan on telling this one twice. I can see the goose flesh crawling up on my arms at just the hint of a thought. So do your business now. Done? Good—we will proceed.

As I said before, no one was living in Foster Manor at the time. I was the only one who had any belongings left, and between work and being with Griffin, I was quite alright just letting the shit sit there for a while. But having found a new house (with its own set of issues, but we will get to that later) and with the need to put the old one up for sale sooner rather than later, I began the arduous process of clearing out my things—probably a bit too lackluster for anyone's taste, but when you have the benefit of a lot of friends at your disposal, you tend to be a bit lackadaisical when it comes to manual labor. So it was a bit piecemeal: a trip here, a trip there, and honestly avoiding almost *all* the big stuff that still had to be moved. I made a solid plan over the next two days to get the remainder out and be done with it. The first night was not so bad. I had rented a truck, and we were putting a solid dent in the removal process. There were some things left for the next night: DVDs (an amount you will remember is substantial), books, odds, ends, a TV, and so forth. I packed up as much as I could so all we would have to do is drop by the next night, pop it all in the truck, and bid adieu. Everything was in boxes and ready to go.

My friends and I assembled the next day at my new house and headed for Foster Manor for the last time. I was not melancholy; I was just ready for the business to be over. As fortune would have it, I arrived before anyone else, so I ran up, unlocked the door, and went inside. I could not believe what I saw when I ran through the entryway. Everything—and I do mean *everything*— had been unpacked and strewn on the floor. Not only had it been pulled out of the boxes we had spent some time packing them in, things like the books and DVDs were stacked in the middle of the fucking living room. Lamps were tipped over. It was fucking bedlam. Now you might think this had been an attempted robbery. But nothing was taken—*nothing*. The TV was still there. Not one movie was gone. More to the point, not one door was jimmied nor one window broken. I checked every possible entrance to the house. It was like someone had thrown a fit, then gotten bored and decided to stack everything just to fuck with my head.

I stared at this insane scene for an eternity. One of my friends turned up and asked what happened. I dejectedly just asked him to help me tidy everything away so we could get out of there. I was done caring about the "what" and the "why" in that place. I just wanted out of the fucker before my head caught fire or pudding shot out my friends' noses. You may laugh, but at that point nothing would have surprised me. We packed the rest of my belongings—or at least the stuff I wanted to keep—into the truck and the other vehicles we had brought, and my friends made their way toward my new digs on the circle. I took a minute, looked around, said goodbye under my breath, and closed that door forever. I have not been back. I even made the realtor come get the keys—I was never going in that place again. Kick the tires on your past so you can make sure you get to the next stop, but do not worry about the mileage. When the time comes to move on, your body knows before your brain does. That is why you always find yourself pointing in a different direction when you did not even realize you had moved.

The end of one life does not mean life ends, period. Life, I have found, is merely a series of changes and adjustments as you work out the kinks and find your true place in the puzzle. Like a sculptor chipping away the bits of the stone to reveal the sculpture beneath the surface, we as men and women slide through the grooves of this crazy record to find the songs that define us, shape us, and make us dance. If that place and time does not feel right, we know it in our bones. The journeys we find ourselves on never necessarily lead to a simple destination; the stops along the way are what get us where we are going. With eyes burnt by the lights we strive to follow, sometimes we are too blind to what is right in front of us, good or bad. It takes a steady breath and a solemn vow to figure out whether or not you have finally come home or you are simply a few blocks away. But I am convinced there is a home out there for all of us. I found mine; time will tell if you truly find yours. But never let yourself be too distracted to notice the sights and the route along the way. If you keep your memories close, your future will never throw you a curve ball. It will just become a series of problems you already know and already possess the means to figure out for yourself.

Now that I have transcribed these events, I will let these memories of Foster Manor subside and rest elsewhere with a sense of lightness that never needs to say its apologies. It was an interesting time in my life, and as I moved on to my next stop in life, there was a part of me that had a vague notion that things like the goings on at Foster Manor would be in my rearview, that the coastline was clear for stronger yet calmer tides. But as I have found out—and to use one of my favorite ironic quotes—"the best way to make God laugh is to announce your plans out loud." Even though I had not said anything, maybe my expectations spoke volumes. I was expecting something more akin to siesta than synergy. However, as I was about to find out, things in my life and indeed in my new house were just about to get even more interesting.

The days of wine and roses were beyond me, and the future was a lock out on the horizon. The time had come for a reevaluation of everything: my goals, my wants, my needs, my vices, my approach to family, parenting, relationships, and who I wanted to be for the next twenty years. I felt for the first time in my life that I was not running from anything but rather was running toward something, something real and worth living for in the end. It was the first step toward the rest of my existence—not something to be taken lightly or for granted. But for over thirty years I had been just another follower who was a little bit more ahead of the curve than others. I wanted the next thirty to be more under my control. The thing is that there is a reason some old clichés are more fact than fiction—they sum up the truth better than anything else. Case in point: the more things change, the more they stay the same.

wine and spirits
with friends

L ET ME ASK YOU SOMETHING before we go any further, because I really do not want to get off on the wrong foot here, and I would be remiss in my duties as a host if I thought to do otherwise. Do *you* know any good ghost stories? I am sure you do—I can see it on your face, slowly biting your lower lip in an attempt to make it less obvious. I wish I could be there in person to transcribe it for use in this naughty haughty tome, but, alas, it is not to be. Therefore, I will give you a little glimpse into one of the deep, dark places that really set this whole thing into motion for me. Grab your security pillow and put down your orange soda—it is time to snuggle up and cast about for that elusive beast known as "the catalyst." This goes back even before I took those first faltering steps into Cold House. Buckle up, bitches.

My mother was born in Arkansas, but eventually she, my uncle, and my grandmother moved to a farm near Knoxville, Iowa, that my Gram owned years before I was even a slight jump of blood in my daddy's pants. However, I am not really sure where this falls in the timeline of my family; I believe this was around the time my grandmother divorced my grandfather. So I am fairly vague when it comes to my knowledge of this time for my family. But I have a very vivid memory of a certain conversation that happened in my presence when I was young, and it had to do with that particular farmhouse. My Gram might smack me in the head for getting it wrong, but it is a great little story. So here you go.

One Sunday my mom, my Gram, and I were on the way to my great grandmother's house, and we happened to pass by this farmhouse. It was an American Horror Story and its subsequent wet dream: painted yellow and kind of drowsy looking; it exuded that back-country vibe of "this space has been here longer than you have lived, and, depending on the weather, it will be here long after you are gone." My Gram and my mom started to talk about life there. Having never heard about this place until that day, I asked what it was like—the place gave me the heebie-jeebies. Someone blurted out, "It was fine until the neighbor was found hanging in his barn. No one knows if it was a suicide or murder, but they say you can still see him in the barn some nights, swinging from the end of his noose." Then, having realized whom they were talking to, they quickly changed the subject. But it was too late; my mind had already envisioned a shadowy figure gently bobbing around on the end of a rope, looking deep into the eyes of the beholder.

That was my first ghost story.

The funny thing is that most of my life people have been regaling me with their paranormal past. When I told my friends what this book would be about, they became energized and wanted to impart to me all of the things they had seen in various locales during their tenures in life. I started to keep a mental catalog so I could include them in this book, because like I said, when you have a good ghost story, that is like a membership into a very exclusive club . . . and membership has its privileges.

One of the first ones I can remember was after I had moved back from Florida to Waterloo, Iowa. I was having a sleepover with some of my friends, and we were joshing and jawing about things and nonsense, just being kids. The weekend was ours, and the sugar was aplenty. So we were just talking good shit and doing whatever boys get up to when they are unfortunately left to their own devices. Then someone—I am not quite sure who, but it does not matter because I am going to change his name—asked the question that usually gets these kinds of balls rolling. For years I have thought about this question and have always conjured up images of kids dressed like gangsters trying to gain egress to a speakeasy: a man with a moustache and a dueling scar slides open a little window high on the door and casually asks, "Password?" We, as whippersnappers, would reply thus: "Do you guys believe in ghosts?"

Everyone in the group that night did—in fact, as I think about it, it slowly morphed into a conversation relatable to who had caught the bigger fish. With each turn, that person tried desperately to one-up the other, to the point at which it had disintegrated into seeing the chupacabra trying to crawl into a window in a trailer park. I let those go, though, because one story jumped out at me immediately. For the sake of respect and privacy, we will call the storyteller Jack.

Jack was a friend of mine who had been horribly burned in a fire that his biological parents had accidentally set when he was very young. Even after several surgeries, Jack was left with multiple scars, loss of hearing in his left ear, and having to sleep with a respirator at night. Vicious people at our school were complete bastards to him, but we had rallied around as best we could, doing our best to shield him from the evil that men (well, kids) do. He was one of us, and we would not suffer lightly the bullshit cast upon him. His foster parents tended to dote and be overprotective, so when they allowed him to come over and spend the night, we tried to make the best of it—as did he. Because of his injuries, Jack had an uncanny ability to plug his nose and whistle out his ears, which, being stupid kids, we absolutely loved. So we knew the more we could make him feel accepted, the better.

That night, while we were swapping ghost stories and squealing on varying levels of horror and disbelief, Jack had gone very quiet. When I asked him what was wrong, he said nothing.

When it came to his turn, he tried to beg off, but we pressed him to give us something. He took a deep breath and simply said, "My parents visit me." We were a little confused: "What do you mean your parents visit you? You live with your parents." He shook his head, soberly—too sober for a boy of his age maybe, but if I had gone through his experiences, maybe I would have felt older too. He sighed and said, "My real parents visit me."

We sat in silence for a second before we forgot that we were dickhead kids and started throwing questions at him: "What do they do?" "What do they say?" "Do they have legs?" "Why would they not have legs, you idiot?" "Some of them float, asshole!" and so on and so forth. We were young and excitable. Jack simply raised a hand. "They never say a word," he said slowly. "They just come into my room or wander the house. Sometimes I wake up and no one is there. Then the next minute there they are. They just watch me. It makes me feel better."

"Do you get scared?"

"No," he said, looking at the floor. "No, honestly I just like it when they are there."

That was the first ghost story I had ever heard in which I got the sense that there was nothing to be afraid of, that maybe we were only scared because we did not understand what they were or why they were there. Jack clearly was not uncomfortable when they were with him—in fact, he smiled while he shared this secret with us. Now some may say it was just wishful thinking on his part and that they were merely in his dreams. Fair play—you could say that. But I was there—I saw his face. I saw his eyes light up as he was explaining it. I could feel his happiness wrap around our little group. No one, at any age, would allow him or herself to be that cruel, even a kid of twelve. Of all the stories I heard that night, Jack's story is the only one that I remember vividly. It was not even a story, really. But he shared that with us because we were his friends, and in a lot of ways that was his most prized possession, his treasured secret. When Jack died a few years later from complications caused by his injuries, the only thing that let me feel okay about it was that maybe he was with them now, visiting others they loved. So maybe they were a dream. But maybe they were really there for him, a little boy saddled with so much so early.

Some of the stories I have been told are just downright goofy. I had a friend who was convinced he had been fucked by a ghost. When I asked him if it was a boy or a girl he became belligerent. "What the hell is that supposed to mean?" he said.

"You just told me that a ghost jumped your bones. But what I just said is over the line? Can you see how that might sound absolutely stupid?"

He said, "It is not my fault if you do not believe in ghosts."

I told him, "Oh, I believe in ghosts. I just do not believe you."

He left.

Subsequently, we did not talk for a while.

That happens to me a lot, now that I think about it. Having said that, however, maybe my prodigious friend was not such a wanker after all. Kesha, the blond-haired singer who desperately wants people to spell her name with a dollar sign (which I fully have the power to do here and have chosen not to because I refuse to enable dipshits), has very recently claimed she had sex with a ghost as well. Jesus on a pita—her too? What the bloody fuck is going on here? And how is it I am missing out on all this ghost sex? I do not believe it, unless . . . my friend is *actually* Kesha after a sex change operation! I *thought* that mess of idiocy coming from the concert speakers was familiar! Good for you, John, I mean Kesha! I still will not buy the paranormal shag claim, but good on ya for reaching for the sky! I just hope I run into you after post-op. That would be an awkward morning-after story, both of us standing at the toilet with piss wood, trying to drain our respective veins.

As I have said, whenever I tell people I am writing this book, the majority of them light up like Blackpool in September, gesturing like mad for me to sit down so they can unload this precarious cargo they have hauled about for the last how-many years. One particular friend, who I will call Mac (because Puddles is a bit cruel), told me about being in a church one night. He and his brother were chased away by a very adamant priest, shushing them and waving them off. They came to find out later from the night watchman that they were the only ones there—no priest was there that late, nor did one live on the premises. Mac is a bit of a skeptic, but even he said that incident made "his old crushed grape pucker up a bit."

On the night in the schoolhouse in Farrar, while we all sat in the Theater Room, we were all going back and forth about our individual experiences. We sat in a circle facing each other with an audio recorder in the middle, its red light subbing for a glowing fire. Too bad we could not roast some s'mores—nothing goes together better than recounting paranormal foreplay and large amounts of high-octane sugary foodstuffs. The gang—composed of myself, The Boss, Lady, Stubs, Truck, Kennedy, Biff, and Knees—sat in the room as the temperature became more and more bipolar, repeating the experiences that had gotten us into paranormal study in the first place. After The Boss and I had taken our turns, respectively, the others were encouraged to do likewise.

Stubs told us of his favorite uncle who had tragically died after a fatal bout with cancer. Stubs said that he always knew when his uncle was over at his parents' house because he would hear him walking up the stairs to his room, his boots stepping heavily on the wood. Well, a few days after his uncle had died, Stubs was in his room when he distinctly heard footsteps coming up his stairs. It sounded just like his uncle's footfalls, so Stubs called out his name. The sound stopped at the door. He ran to see who it was, and there was no one there. If that fails to make the hairs on your nuts stand straight up, you either have no nuts, shave them regularly, or you are made of sturdier stuff than I am.

Biff's story is just as chilling. Biff works in the funeral industry and wears many hats: director, embalmer, cremator, aesthetics, and so on. She has even been known to help load the unfortunately deceased into the limos and hearses from time to time. It was on one of these occasions that she had just seen to a customer's transport when a person stepped up to the hearse to peer through the window. She politely chastised the person, explaining that the family would not appreciate it and that this was a time for respect, not voyeurism. The person ignored her. Biff turned away for half a second, fully intending to return her attention to the disrespectful gatecrasher. But when she returned her attention to the miscreant, he had vanished. Now Biff had never given a second thought to the existence of spirits before that day. But since then her opinions have changed, as you can imagine.

The others had varying degrees of commonality: Knees had a pretty harrowing encounter in a hotel room in Colorado with a door that inexplicably closed violently by itself. Truck had no prior experiences but had a slight NDE (near-death experience) while serving in the Army. It was plain to see that we had all had a brush with abnormality in some way or another. Maybe this is why I get so infuriated when so-called realists come off so high and mighty about how such things cannot be real. How can all these people be wrong? How can we all be lying? How can we all share these instances and still be mild-mannered civilians? I do not dismiss anything in life without good reason. It took me years to slam the door on religion, even though from the start something stank in Denmark. I at least gave the opportunity for the counterpoint to be made. Of course it did not work so well for the opposing debate team. Maybe that is why so many people shut down at the very hint that this may in fact have some weight and credence. There are impenetrable minds and opaque points of view; maybe the best thing to do is not try to knock in some windows but instead sail a few notes over the battlements.

Let me tell you about an actual period in my life when I was considered a "Goth." It started in Des Moines when I was in my early twenties and continued until I was around twenty-seven. For anyone unfamiliar with this particular fad, it involves (or involved at the time) pale makeup, eyeliner, black clothing, and a style of shirt known as a "poet's shirt," though it looked more like it was fit for a pirate or a musketeer. It also was very important to have the ability to imbibe as much alcohol as humanly possible. I discovered that all Goths were drunks, and it led to my abandoning the fashion because I realized I did not have to go to all that trouble with the eyeliner and the gear just to get fucked up; I could put on a hat and go to a bar—less trouble, really. But during that time I met some amazing people, especially when I moved to Denver, Colorado, and started going to a Goth club called the Wreck Room, which occupied the basement of a building at 1082 Broadway.

The club itself was unfinished and dark, unseemly if you were a civilized human. But for us Goths, it was a paradise of shadowy corners and black lights, My Life with the Thrill Kill Cult blasting through hidden speakers and people trying a little too hard to look like Tom Cruise in *Interview with a Vampire* while strolling around drinking *really* spooky drinks like 7 and 7s or shots of Jager. Yes, it was pompous and embarrassing at times. But I loved it so much, and my friends were a real crew of miscreants. I had a friend named Mr. Nipples who I have talked about in the past, and we ran together in the Goth crowd—we even moshed to "Angel of Death" at the Wreck Room, much to the chagrin of the other patrons. We were just a little more fucked up than most of these walking billboards for Anne Rice. Maybe it was because we both came from Iowa. Maybe it was because we both had similar experiences.

Mr. Nipples and I both had run-ins with black shapes, human by visage but very horrific, like silhouettes in 3D. One had chased him when he was younger, and he revealed in a fairly amusing story how he had jumped out of the back of a pickup and tried to basically hulk out on it. If I am not mistaken, I believe his correct words were "vamp out" on it. Then he roared at me while flying two fists full of devil horns in my direction. That was a very strange Thursday, to say the least. I guess when you are in a state of fright, you either run or you fight; that impulse is in all of us. The way he told the story made me smile, but I understood the undercurrents of it. I had felt like there was something following me all my life. I had deduced that it all came back to that night when my friends and I had invaded Cold House. But I could never be sure. Certainly, as I will explain later, some of my more "sensitive" friends are convinced that some spirits have glommed onto me and have followed me from the Foster Manor to our current house, somewhere in the wilds of West Des Moines. I do not know if this is true, but I can tell you this: I never really feel alone. This could be paranoia or a turd in my pocket—your guess is as good as mine.

There is a different side of the parking lot to this story as well. I have certain friends who refuse to even discuss this subject for fear of something coming back into their lives. It is very disconcerting: one minute we are having a clear-cut, terrific talk, and the next thing you know, the wrong thing is said, and their force field comes down like on an episode of *Star Trek*. No one comes in and no one gets out—just a stern look and an icy silence. When the tension subsides enough that I can finally get a word in, these friends will only talk about why—not the where, when, and what. It is genuinely like a paranormal witness relocation program. They will only tell me that extraordinary things occurred, people were terrified and hurt, thankfully the incidents stopped, and they do not wish to jinx the peace out of respect to their loved ones. Of course, this only furthers my curiosity. But I respect their issues—that shit can cling to you like cat hairs on a black suit. There is no getting away from it, and there is also every possibility it will get into your food. Or something like that—I might have to reassess my parables.

One such friend was a man I will call Frank. He had a handful of experiences in an old two-story house he had rented on the east side of Des Moines. I believe it was built in the 1920s, but I could be wrong; what I do know is that it was near the fairgrounds and a part of what we called Old Town, because that side of the city was the seat of industry in those days. However, when most of the refineries and factories moved outside of town, the area fell into despair financially, and eventually it became a bit seedy and dilapidated. This meant that there were several wonderfully quaint houses that you could rent for fairly cheap. Frank found such a house with his then-girlfriend and moved in with another couple to share the rent. It was a bit shabby: there were things left over from the previous tenants, like old blankets and a beat-up old tricycle that they stored in the downstairs closet. But with some TLC and a little bit of spare paint, they had managed to adapt this relic into a home of sorts. But as all things in this book, it was then that things got really interesting. Almost immediately things started to happen, he said. Pots and pans banged together in the middle of the night. Children laughed and cried in the house, but there were no children living there— not even young relatives. Frank was at his wit's end, and his girl-friend was determined to move. The crazy thing was that the other roommates *ignored it*. They wrote it off with the standard J-11 excuse of "there has to be a reasonable explanation," blah blah blah. They did not even want to talk about it; they were very much in denial about the whole thing.

One night that all changed dramatically.

The two couples were sitting in the living room, shooting the shit and having a beer. They had all had really long days at work and welcomed the chance to kick their shoes off and just relax for a few minutes. Being that they all enjoyed each other's com-pany, it was a nice little evening for the four of them. They were just about to switch the TV on when they heard the laughter from upstairs again. Frank had had enough and tried to call the other couple to the carpet: "How do you explain that?" he said. "How do you suppose that is happening? There are absolutely no kids here—what is making that noise then?" The other gentle-man kindly reminded them that there may be younger kids who live next door and that they may very well be hearing echoes from the other house through an open window somewhere up-stairs. My guess is that the supernatural has an excellent sense of timing, because the man had not even finished his dissertation when that beat-up old tricycle rolled itself into the living room completely on its own and stopped dead in their midst. It did not, however, come to rest after using up its inertia; it hit the brakes and stopped, as if two little feet had been pedaling and decided that was where it wanted to sit. There were several seconds of stunned silence. Then the other couple got up, went to bed . . . and moved out the next day. Frank and his girl did the same a day later.

The reason I tell you this story is because it eventually ruined their relationship. Frank and his girlfriend did not break up because they wanted to or because they had grown to hate each other or even because they had fallen out of love with each other; they broke up because they felt it was the only solution they could think of to rid each other of this persistent presence. The way Frank put it, these things followed them from that house to every subsequent dwelling they chose to have together. It got to be so intolerable that it drove them apart. And once they split up, these things stopped happening. So Frank and this woman made a decision that it was in their best interests to never have any contact again out of fear that "the kids would come back and want to play again." I listened to this story in amazement. I started thinking about my ideas on "intelligent energy" and wondered if certain energies were attracted to each other. Certainly electrons cable themselves together in attracted bundles and quarks could do the same thing. Maybe that explains why certain people and their respective souls feel so drawn to one another and experience painful emptiness when they are apart. If this were true for living people, why not spirits? Maybe they sense a sort of sameness or consistency in unique individuals that makes them go crazy, and they cannot help but be around them. Maybe in Frank's case it was the combined energy of him and his ex that kept those precocious dead scamps coming back around. Now these two love-birds refuse to be together because it was all too much to bear.

It is one of the saddest stories I have ever heard, but in between the lines there is a romantic sentiment, akin to soul mates and kindred spirits. God, I could not imagine being away from my wife in a case like that—I would go mad. I would rather suffer through a poltergeist than be away from her, plain and simple. I will take flying pots and pans over separation from The Boss any day. Sometimes you have to ask yourself which hell would you rather succumb to: the one in which the outside forces seem to be after you, or the one in which the one you love cannot be with you? Both options are not what you might call awesome, and I would not wish that kind of decision on anyone.

That may explain the kids on the circle, which we will get to later on. Maybe that is why they are still around, because they feel a kinship with me. It may be why that darkness had followed me through the years as well. Energetic attraction: what a fucking concept, eh? Shit, I have said too much. You will just have to wait for more on that in a little bit.

For some weird reason I am reminded of a particular Halloween in 2002, back when my hair was dyed black, I was sixty pounds heavier, I drank a lot, and "Bother" was getting a lot of airplay on the radio. We were on the road with Stone Sour at the time, promoting the self-titled first album. Unbeknownst to me, someone at the record label had involved me in a radio contest for a Seattle station in which one lucky winner got a sponsored Halloween party for their friends . . . and I would show up and play "Bother" in their living room. I had no idea this had been planned, executed, and arranged. But about a week before Halloween, I got wind of this and kind of flipped out. In order for me to make this happen I would have to play a show, leave the tour, fly into Seattle, do the Halloween party, sleep for fifteen minutes, turn around, and fly back for another show the next day. Halloween was my only day off. Now I had been obligated to show up for a party with god knows whomever and try not to suck, all on about ten minutes sleep.

No pressure.

It is not that I did not think it was a cool idea—it was a cool idea. I just hate surprises, especially surprises that add work to an already gnarly work schedule. I rolled with the clichéd punches and did my best to keep a stiff upper lip for the occasion. I also did my best not to get completely blotto before the thing because I was going to a stranger's house sight unseen, and I wanted to do my best. So I put on my nicest long-sleeved shirt, threw on my Jack Skellington hat, grabbed my acoustic, and headed for the airport. That leg of the shit was fine. It was once I got to Seattle that things started to go awry for yours truly.

The label rep picked me up around 7 P.M. and said it would be a bit of a drive. An hour later we were still driving. I had no idea the deepest recesses of the Congo extended all the way to Washington State. I had given up hope of ever seeing civilization again when we suddenly turned off the pavement onto a gravel road that disappeared into the wilderness. Flashes of *Last House on the Left* flew through my head—the original, not the remake, although the remake was not half bad. As we got further and further away from the lights of the city, both my hope and my enthusiasm were dissipating. It turned out we were lost. We had to backtrack a bit, and then suddenly there was a row of houses that seemed to have grown up in the middle of nowhere. By houses, I really mean *mansions*. These were high-end family escapes away from the urban grind.

I was expected to perform in one of their living rooms.

We entered the winner's house and two things struck me at once, and both made me want to run for my life. One, everything in this house looked like it cost a million fucking dollars. Just out of self-preservation I did not want to touch anything; if these people sued me, I would owe them money after death. Two, I found myself surrounded by a contingent of hopped-up teenagers, all decked in costumes, ready to *party with Corey Taylor*. Jesus, Mary, and Joseph, this was going to be a long night.

They set me up in the corner of the living room on a wooden bar stool, with an intern from the radio station trying in vain to get a very modest PA system to work so I could sing for these people. The speakers themselves were about the size of two packs of cigarettes and sounded about as savory. Finally, we jettisoned the PA idea in favor of having everyone there crowd around so they could hear me clearly. It was a surreal scene out of Spinal Tap: to my right were the radio people, to my left was my label representative, immediately in front of me were all the costumed folk, and behind them were all the parents, staring in disbelief that any of these kids gave a bear's fart about the fat Goth in the beanie with the guitar. I played my song and a couple others, retired my gig fiddle to its case, and went directly to the kitchen, where the parents were guarding the alcohol.

The rest of the night is a befuddling blur. After fifteen minutes the parents and I were doing shots of Canadian Club, challenging each other to see how many we could do inside thirty seconds. Within an hour I was so shit-faced I was back in the living room teaching the youngsters how to do "The Time Warp" from *Rocky Horror Picture Show*, which was on VH1. I have no idea when I left or how I got back to my hotel room, but when I came to, the sun was up, my pillow was stuck to my face, and a very confused housekeeper had ignored my "DO NOT DISTURB" sign, leaning over me and asking me in broken English if I wanted turn-down service. To put it mildly, I did not.

I cannot even remember why I told you that story. I know there was a reason, but now that reason has escaped my Nerf-like brain. You know what? Give me til the end of this chapter—I am sure it will come back to me. Either that or I will end up wandering the house in my Doctor Who pajamas picking at my gums with a no. 2 pencil and talking to the dust particles swarming around my head in a vain attempt to communicate with their kind. I am here to tell you: too much coffee in the morning makes for very strange habits when no one else is paying attention. But I suspect there might be some interesting YouTube footage coming your way if my family planted hidden cameras around that place. I will be the first to say it: I apologize . . . and my family is a bunch of bastards.

Just when I thought things would never get as weird as I had already discovered, it just went ahead and fucking did without asking.

I have homes in Des Moines, where my kids and grandmother live, and Las Vegas, where my family on my wife's side live. I split time between the two, but lately I have been spending more time in Las Vegas because, as the paternal catalyst, I have a responsibility to my married side to come take up too much space on the couch and occasionally kill a spider. Just recently we moved into a new house in a very nice neighborhood, with more space and speed bumps and everything. It felt like a proper place to raise kids and have dinners with family friends—all the stuff you do when you are either getting older or looking for an investment property or both. I was very excited myself because the place came with recessed speaker systems in every room and a pool table—you know, the important stuff. So we eagerly moved in. The house directly across the street was empty, but some of the neighbors on either side waved, smiled, and made us feel pretty good as we shoved all our stuff into our new home. There was parking for almost everyone (which is no easy feat—there are a lot of us) and a wonderful backyard. It was perfect in every way.

Then the "empty" house across the street turned out to be not so empty.

When you peek inside the windows, it looks innocuous enough: just a collection of big, empty pseudo-adobe rooms painted Southwestern Peach in an attempt to give it that modern rustic feel. There is not a scrap of furniture in the joint, not even a remnant abandoned in haste because there was no room left on the truck for anything else. It is flat-out un-fucking-lived in. But every other night, 8 P.M. until 11 P.M., that house turns into some sort of crazy rave-like TV party. There are eerie blue lights that illuminate the upstairs rooms and hallways, concentrating in the upper living room area. It looks like a group of Gremlins are dragging twenty-five-inch plasmas around while tripping on massive tabs of E. I have seen it with both eyes, and it is fucked up. These events are punctuated with *really* loud fucking noises as well, like a rugby match between Australia and Great Britain just across the street and everything is on the line. It is fucking out of control over there, and it just keeps getting weirder and weirder. Shit is starting to bleed into our house now, with unexplained activity going on in the west part of the damn house. What the hell am I going to do with *another* fucked up house? Am I supposed to wander around with invisible vittles and treat this like an undead soiree? James fucking Francis, I cannot win!

To sum up this chapter, I find myself thinking about more than just the tales I have been told and the various chats I have been privy to over the years. You see, if you have not already fig-ured it out, I am very much an extroverted social vessel who loves nothing more than to drink shit tons of coffee and chew the metaphorical fat with me and mine, my collection of crazy iconoclasts that I have surrounded myself with for what feels like centuries. I have always been fascinated by tales of the Algo-nquin Round Table from yesteryear, an amazing confluence of intellect and personalities that saw the likes of Dorothy Parker, Will Rogers, and others trading barbs over dinners and dexter-ous displays of heady witticisms. In my life I have had these same types of moments, going all the way back to 1992 when we the people could invade a Perkins Restaurant at midnight, plunk down a dollar for a bottomless pot of coffee (split among twelve people), smoke our asses off for hours, and just talk good shit until the sun came up. Those are truly some of my most cher-ished memories—traversing the psyches of my fabulous friends, who were just as fucked up and brilliant as I was, jotting down notes on receipts, writing lyrics on McDonald's applications, dis-covering ways to make every dream you ever had come true. I can recall nearly every conversation that occurred at those tables and in those booths. I had not just found my place in the world; I found myself in that particular world. I saved myself from that clichéd and depressed destruction most crazy geniuses find when they are young. The damnable tragedy is that I will never get to thank those long-lost friends for helping me get through it all. So I go on, moving through different talks into this place we call the future, feeling the road more than seeing it, because to me that is so much more rewarding once you reach your des-tination.

Ultimately that is what this chapter is: a way to collect these spirit-laden yarns together for posterity while simultaneously offering a subtle little dedication to those souls out there who helped mold me, shape me, chisel me out of pure attitude and profundity into the glorious fuck up I am today. I want them to know I am doing my best to carry on those conversations, to continue that Silly String Theory we loved so much back then. That, to me, is the real proof of relativity: time may not exist forward, but I can trace my own back across the years with the help of the safety line provided by a thousand pure hours of smiling cogitation and wild-eyed postulation, solving world hunger and starting fake bands, being a man and learning to love women and vice versa or both. Things like convention matter so little when the world is new to you. All that really matters is finding a place in that world that feels like no one else was there before you. Nothing kills ingenuity like that tired sense that maybe you are just repeating someone else and their fading footsteps. Therefore, I use these memories to track the unexplained and the undiscovered because they were and remain wonderful, they were and remain eloquent and irreverent, and they are very much alive in my minefield of a mind.

My kitchen table has replaced that Perkins Restaurant. I draw people in like a vegan spider to rip through their creative bends and offer my own inspiration to them in return for a blast of quickened curiosity. Sure, I certainly do not enjoy them as often as I used to; I am, of course, the workaholic machine that is Corey Fuckin' Taylor after all, and I have shit to do every spare second not spent allowing myself to inexplicably go unconscious for another round of sleep cycles. But I still have great friends who I like to verbally joust with at every stolen opportunity. It definitely keeps me interested in this sadly banal and barren place called Earth, and it helps me accrue things like the different ghost stories some of us have dragged behind us for years, suddenly ready to dump them off to share with the world. I had a simile here about new shoes at a Salvation Army drop box, but I really do not feel that is correct, because we are not letting go of them; we are surely only sharing them with the rest of the class. At a time when so many of us are so desperately trying to find ways to connect with the rest of the aberrant cell divisions called humans, why not try something like sitting down and *talking*? And if you are talking, why not try *sharing*? And if you are sharing, why not share a bit about something as exciting and polarizing as *ghosts*? Just a thought . . .

By the time you read this, I will be miles away from here, looking for my next excursion and plotting more creative ways to fuck with your heads. I might be dressed nicely; I might also be in that nice tutu number I wore in London on Halloween back in 2010. You really never know when it comes to what the hell goes on in my frosted flaky crust of a brain. But I can definitely tell you one thing: I am always looking for a great conversation, because at the end of the day I am a collector who overdoes it at every turn. If I love it, I will go above and beyond to add it to the Vault. I keep the great conversations in a very special hellish place inside that I can access at will, kind of like a pleasure memory palace. In there, nothing is off limits, nothing is over the limit, and nothing is limited. The only way is all the way, as I have been known to say in the past. But if you are worth it, I will collect you. I will add you to my history. Maybe some day I will add you to pages like these. I believe that everyone needs to live forever, because no single life is better or worse than the other. Maybe that is my endgame in all this.

My friends gave me these personal ghost stories so that I might share them with you, hopefully to encourage and enable you to do that likewise with your friends. By doing this, not only do you prove that none of us are alone; you also carry on that wonderful conversation I adore—the one that stretches across the years, never wavers or falters, and yet brings us closer to happiness than anything else has yet in life. We are our own treasured historians. We are our own witnesses to what we have done. When you share that with someone else, the chances of being remembered improve exponentially. This is the true key to immortality. This is the belt loop that will hold together the fabric of what is real and what is imagined to blend this tapestry into the rest of this world.

So . . . know any good ghost stories?

A HAUNTING IN
NEW YORK?

RAPIDS
Theatre

THE OLD SAYING has always been "necessity is the mother of invention." I have found this to be true on several occasions, not only for the many inspired creations that I see on a nightly basis when it comes to the sensation that is "As Seen on TV," but I myself have reveled in the concept a time or two. Sometimes I get more done when I know there is a hard deadline and I have no clue as to what is next. Suddenly the paranoia and panic hits you like a handful of frozen cow shit. And then the miraculous happens: a trigger clicks, the wheels spin themselves out of the muddy thought process, and you are off and running, typing away like a madman or fervently scribbling lyrics and music in mystic notebooks like a wizard on crack who was able to recall an incantation thought lost aeons ago. It is a beautiful thing when you remember you happen to be really clever—at least when your brain gets out of its own way.

Ironically this is the crux of where I happened to be while I was working on this book. I was all but finished writing, had gone and shot most of these weird photos you see within, and was busy clearing up any refuse clinging to this hunk of wood pulp and ink. I was jovial and elated—book two was nearly in the bag. Who would have thought I would be putting the final touches on *another* book? For fuck's sake, I was still pinching myself over getting away with the first one. So this was more due diligence than victory lap—time to kick the tires, air them up, and make sure the lug nuts were on nice and tight. But in doing so, I realized this vicious bastard of a book was in fact . . . not long enough. What the fuck . . . not long enough? How could it be that I, the Great Big Mouth, the One and Only Motherfucker, was at a loss for words? Had I sustained some sort of wicked blow to the cerebellum? Never mind all that shit—had I been hit on the head? What the French, totes?

Of course, I knew the problem. I had scheduled another ghost hunt, and because I am "busier than a one-legged man in an ass-kicking contest" (you can thank Geoff Head for that wonderfully visual quote), I had been forced to cancel a trip at the last minute to the Squirrel Cage Jailhouse in Omaha, Nebraska, even after they had graciously made arrangements contrary to their operating hours. So with much chagrin, I thanked them for their kindness, begged out of the engagement, and decided I would have ample verbiage for the tome you are currently cradling between your groceries and your purse—at least that is what I imagine you have it stuck in. Anywhere else is either gross, illegal, or out of my experience circle. Anyway, I was a little light in the chapters and unable to reschedule the Squirrel Cage Jailhouse or anywhere else for that matter. What in the name of Odin's soul patch was I going to do?

Thankfully, necessity was about to give birth to my salvation. On January 22, 2013, I woke up in the literally freezing but spiritually warm city of Buffalo, New York, and prepared myself for the second night of the House of Gold and Bones US tour. The boys in Stone Sour and I were thrilled to be out on the road, especially Johnny Chow that day—this was his hometown, and his whole family would be making the chilly trek to see him perform that night at the Rapids Theatre in Niagara Falls, not too far away from Buffalo. We were ecstatic—the tour was already off to a grand start and expectations were very high. In my time on the road I could not recall if I had ever played the Rapids Theatre, so to me it was just one more venue I could add to my list of recollections. That was before I got a provocative text from The Boss, who was already at the gig setting things up. "The club is supposedly haunted, so you will have more material for your book," she matter-of-factly stated.

Really? Interesting . . .

A haunting in New York? Color me stoked. This was perfect—I could kill two birds with one stone. Play an awesome gig in a pretty historical building *and* go on a ghost hunt, all while staying on schedule and fulfilling my quota at the same glorious time. I could not believe my luck, really. I kept waiting for the catch, but it never came. I could work *and* investigate. Plus, I did not have much press, so I could spend most of the night running around the club, taking it all in and waiting for something spooky to happen. That is the thing about kismet: just when you think the universe will never realign in your favor, a pebble out in space bounces off a forgotten Russian satellite and clears a path straight to your face with enlightenment, opportunity, and a little lucky "fuck yeah." That is exactly what the universe was giving me in that one moment between pajamas and blue jeans: an opportunity to catch up when before there was only the Hoover Dam of calamities. Good thing karma and I are on immaculate speaking terms right now.

I immediately packed my things, checked out of the hotel in haste, and raced to the venue. Being a whore for content, before I left I went online and did some slick-quick research, just to get my bearings on this new little wrinkle I would be adding to my sticky skin. Luckily, there was a Wikipedia page. Is it just me, or does it seem like everyone and their fucking mom has a Wikipedia page these days? Shit, even William Hung still has a page on that bastard website. Is it really necessary to know the complete history of the Twinkie? I thought that was what the show *How It's Made* was for. Note to self: look into frivolous use of Wikipedia entries for redundancy and rampant pointlessness. Shit, where was I . . .

The Rapids Theatre was originally built and opened way back in 1921 under the moniker "The Bellevue Theater." In its early heyday it was both a movie theater and a vaudeville house, hosting the acts of the day and showing various big cinematic hits when they would roll through town. But as my digging progressed, I unearthed that this particular venue had gone through a lot of different names over the ninety-plus years in its tenure. It would open, close, and reopen under many different owners, with a plethora of assorted names: the Late Show Discotheque, the Masquerade, Centre Stage, the Pleasure Dome, then just the Dome Theater. People seemed willing to pay any price to own the place as well: one person bought at $18,000, and yet another procured it for $85,000. In 2009 it was finally renovated at a nice nifty sum and renamed the Rapids Theatre. Maybe this shifty and piecemeal story is why the tales of the paranormal are fairly succinct.

The prevalent story that seems to be where all this ghostly talk comes from is the one about a scorned actress who purportedly hung herself in the rafters in the back of the theater. Her spirit is said to roam the halls of the theater, giving glimpses to bystanders and walking the stage when the lights are low and no one is around. There is a bit of contention about what the real stressor for the suicide seemed to be: one legend maintained it was merely a lover who had left her for another woman, another said it was her fiancé, and still another made it clear it was her estranged husband. The only tidbit these versions have in common is that she had been pregnant and unfortunately lost the child. However, in all my research, I found no news report that said anything of the sort regarding *any* version of the tale. Something like that most certainly would have appeared in the papers.

But there is no mention of such a terrible occurrence anywhere. So this might just be an old wives' tale that has been passed down from owner to owner, staff to staff. That tracks more than a horribly sad suicide that slipped through the cracks between buyouts. The stories persist, though, because apparently the presence of something above and beyond is very real. Shadows move where no one was. Whistling can be heard floating through the complex. Footsteps race around the hardwoods and behind people. One of the security guards talked about slipping and almost falling before invisible hands suddenly caught and righted him. Having a little in common with something like that, I was inclined to believe that one.

Another security guard showed me pictures from when the theater was new, with its sprawling seating area and lush balconies. It looked nothing like it does today. I believe the rows of theater chairs were taken out years ago. In the middle of the floor the new owners have built an elaborate wooden bar area, replete with a towering bar back that doubles as a lighting desk. That does not make much sense, seeing as that should be where the sound engineer goes (they stuck our man Big Shirt off to the left of stage, which made the Brit piss himself with rage and incredulity), but I do not own the place. All I really know is that of all the acts and movies that have blown through this joint, we are by far the most recent—although I cannot help but think we are not the first to complain about the placement of our light and sound.

The building had also housed a few other businesses in its time, like a dentist's office and an attorney-at-law. Apparently the dentist decided not to leave, because he is purportedly one of the haunts who traipse through the darkened hallways. The other, according to the locals, is Howard the projectionist. Howard's father owned a business nearby and was connected to the theater for decades, holding the job of projectionist for years until he passed away. The folks who work the Rapids have several pictures that show a multicolored orb they are convinced is Howard himself. The orb resembles an old kaleidoscope, with the main colors of a tube TV screen: red, blue, and green. It is always in the background—it does not appear to want any attention. It just feels like it wants to observe and be near people. Harmless, I guess. Howard the projectionist comes back as a rainbow orb that is attracted to human contact in the very place he used to work. Art imitating life I have heard of; souls imitating skills is another thing entirely.

It makes sense—some people are defined by what they do. Why would it not stand to reason that your spirit might be literally defined by who and what you were in life? I like that scenario the most because it backs up my idea of why spirits might become connected to certain houses or places—because it is the place that brought them the most joy in life, not necessarily that they had to have died violently or suddenly on those specific premises. So when they slip through the veil and their energy refuses to pass on, it is drawn to that special place, maybe as a way to keep that energy reacting to the emotion as a strange type of "recharge." I feel another hypothesis developing in a train of thought that already has too many damn passengers. Trust me—this is not the first time I have considered the idea that I desperately need a hobby.

As the security guard kept scrolling through the photos, I saw several that had fiery orbs racing through the frames, like balls of hellfire being hurled by an invading army toward castle walls. I was struck by how vivid they appeared to be, especially when you considered they were taken in near pitch-black darkness. I casually asked about it and whether there was any info concerning where it had come from. He shrugged and said, "No one really knows. But we think it has something to do with one of the shadow people." When I asked another person who worked at the theater about it, her eyes got wide. "That is a bad one," she said, "It goes where it wants and does what it wants around here."

The Bad One was a mystery almost as intriguing as the actress's supposed suicide. Nobody had any information about it, not even an educated guess as to who or what it had been in life, let alone where the thing had come from. All they knew was that it seemed to stir itself when there was an event or a show going on. The security guard told me that during a Stone Temple Pilots concert there was even video of the thing pushing its way through the mosh pit and concertgoers looking at each other accusingly, like "why the fuck you pushing, bro?" Something that could go back and forth between orb and shadow form while also having the mass to push people when it was moving had to have a lot of energy and emotion behind it. The locals also thought it was responsible for various shoving and pushing that would happen around the complex, nearly spilling someone from a ladder a few years ago during the renovation periods. But the question remains: what the hell is this thing, and where in blue fuck did it come from?

Over the theater's life it has been a number of businesses and served many purposes, so it stands to reason that in its history there may have been a period or periods that made the place privy to some nefarious activity, possibly when it was a discotheque or a jazz club. Something may have happened there years ago, and all the recent action on the grounds causes this spirit to manifest strongly. It could be that this place had some meaning in the person's life and it returned here out of spite or whatnot. This is all conjecture, of course. I have no idea of the story on this place any further than what I have found on websites and what employees have told me. So anything past that is a guess, educated or otherwise, and usually the latter. Who knows what the Bad One really is? The real disturbing question is: what is it going to do next time?

There is that intelligent part of me that knows there really is nothing to be afraid of. These beings—if that is what they are—probably have no idea what they are doing or if they are hurting anyone. But a gun has no idea it is a killing machine. A virus has no idea it can destroy its host. A long fall is an action not a thought. Some things are just what they are, whether they are dangerous or inane. Nature has a way of finding work for everything, kind of like a temp service of this strange world we all troll through. If there is a purpose for these phenomena, maybe we just have not discovered it yet. That explains a lot, seeing as I still have no idea why mosquitoes exist. Bloodsucking, smarmy, disease spreading, larvae-laying, greedy . . . sorry. I have a lot of anger toward those gross, tiny, filthy, fucking bastards. They must think I have sugar in my blood, because they are always after my delicious ass.

I really need to look into ADD medication . . .

I made plans to take a guided tour of the supernatural "hot spots" after the gig so I could get more in depth, maybe even see something with my own eyes, whether it was a shadow or a gas bubble. I mean that *could* be what all the hubbub was about—electrical interference on the human body. It has been proven that when you spend too much time around faulty wiring or open outlets with improper housing, the electromagnetic waves can cause paranoia, uneasiness, and headaches. It has been known to cause hallucinations as well. So when you find yourself suddenly immersed in the effects of a bad electrical installation for an extended period of time, strange things can happen to the faculties. Something gave me the sneaking suspicion that in a building that was built in the 1920s and had also gone through god knows how many renovations, there may be a reason other than the paranormal for the things that everyone was seeing. You see, I do not just accept blindly—I question until I find the natural end of the conversation. I make up my own mind. Maybe there was something there. Maybe someone with a headache jumped at his or her own shadow.

We played the gig, and it was killer. Unfortunately, I spent half the damn time waiting for a shadow man to go streaking through the crowd, knocking over dude bros like bowling pins on a 7-10 split. I was waiting for anything: a speaker to fall, an orb in the strobe lights, a harmony from beyond the grave. . . . To my sadness, none of that happened. But then again, what the hell had I really expected? A ghost trying to stage dive? A literal Wall of Death? This is what I mean by expectations—I did not want to know anything about the schoolhouse in Farrar for this same reason. My imagination was running the show—nothing I was going to see would be righteous. I would never know if it was real or conjured from my brain.

I have to be honest: I did not know why I was acting this way. It was not like this was my first haunted venue. I had been playing places like the Eagle's Ballroom in Milwaukee, Wisconsin, for over a decade now, and *that* fucking place would give even Stone Cold Steve Austin the heebie-jeebies. I had heard stories about the Eagle's Ballroom since I had first played there back in 1999, that it had been a gentlemen's club for German spies back in the thirties, and the ghosts of Nazi sympathizers had been haunting the place ever since. I had also heard that it had been a makeshift children's hospital during an influenza epidemic and that the spirits of some of the children who had not made it still moved about on the lower levels where the pool was operated. I had even seen things happen down in that pool area with my own eyes. I had played there on my solo/book tour; my dressing room had been down in the bowels of the club. On my way to stage I had passed a giant mirror that was mounted on one of the walls, and in that mirror, across the empty pool, I saw three children in nightgowns staring at me. When I whipped my head around to see where they were standing, they had vanished. Needless to say I was a little off my game that night at the gig. Most old clubs just have the usual in their dressing rooms: old posters, furniture, complimentary shitty tea or coffee, and the occasional dick drawn crudely on the walls. The Eagle's Ballroom certainly had a little more to offer than that.

In fact, the day we played the Eagle's Ballroom on the same tour, several little things had happened that had added up to a lot of big strong men acting like eight-year-olds. Johnny Chow had been playing his bass near a giant wooden door that was propped open with a nice sturdy wedge. I happened to be standing at the top of a set of stairs nearby. Johnny looked up at our drum tech, Stewart, to say hello, and as his back was turned, the giant door slammed shut. It did not get loose from its wedge and it was not pushed by any of us. The fucking thing slammed itself shut—against the wedge, which was still jammed at the bottom of the door—and did so *loudly*. It scared all kinds of fuck out of us. But that was just the start of the night's entertainment. While the band and I were upstairs doing a meet and greet with some fans, our sound guy, Big Shirt, was down in the smoking dressing room, by himself and just chilling out. No one else was in that area. He said that out of nowhere he heard the sound of keys rustling in a door lock, vigorously. This went on for a bit until it slowly stopped. Then, in clear view, he watched as an invisible hand pulled on a tablecloth on one of the hospitality tables. It almost yanked a lava lamp onto the floor. When we walked back into the room, he was bug-eyed and white as a bleached sheet. He told us what had occurred, then left in a state of shock. I loved it—more to feed to my book, I said to myself. I was going to have to come to the Eagle's Ballroom more often! The key here was none of that affected my gig that night in any way, shape, or form. It had not even crossed my mind while I was up on the stage, and I did not spend half the show searching for "crowd surfers" who had not paid to get in, so to speak.

So why was I so full of expectation here in Niagara Falls, New York? It might have been a plethora of things. I was on the clock hard up against a deadline. I had been promised a slew of examples that I had not experienced myself yet. I was excited and giddy about playing a show for someone who might or might not be among the living. Who knows? Maybe I was just caught up in the moment, and when you find yourself stuck in that trap, even when you get exactly what you were hoping for, it never seems to leave you satisfied. Humanity has such a propensity for need that an ocean of more can never fill its endless reservoir. At the end of the day I suppose I know more about ghosts and paranormal activity than I do about human nature . . . and that may be a sad state of affairs when one realizes it to be true.

Long story short (too late), after the show I washed my face and balls, got dressed, and realized I really did not have time for the ghost tour. The next show was in that city that never lets me sleep—New York City. I had a press list that made my eyes water in pain: I can tell you now that I did not get done with that damn press list until an hour and a half before the show, by which time I was so completely wiped out I almost had no memory of the gig itself. So knowing the next day was going to be murder on all five of my senses, I opted out of the spooky tour, thanked the security guard for making time to do so, collected my shit, and made for the bus. I had mixed feelings in my bag. Part of me was exhausted and wanted desperately to sack out in my bunk with the Investigation Discovery channel. The other part was a bit bummed out. I had been on a wave of enthusiasm all that day because it was going to make for great text, but at the end of it all I was just too shot to engage in the adventure. Was I getting too old for this shit? Hey, if Danny Glover was, I could be as well. Was I losing the mood? Did I need to start taking those tacky artificial testosterone pills I saw on every other commercial that promised a better golf game and guaranteed a threesome in the bedroom every night? That would be rich: me running around a darkened theater with a half-cocked raging boner yelling, "Fore!" Sometimes I definitely scare myself, no spirits required.

Suffice it to say, I have no big wrap-up party for the Rapids Theatre like I did for the Farrar Schoolhouse. No cake and coffee, no evidence to sift through, no bell book or candle—just a very strange day of riders on the storm, waiting patiently for the extraordinary to occur. But just when I thought all was lost, a little nugget from the grave sent me to rest with a thought that the impossible might just be possible if you stick around after the credits for an Easter egg full of continuous legends. After all the positive anxiety and expectation, this gave me a rare moment to reflect on the fact that maybe, just maybe, there was someone looking out for me. Maybe not the Coca-Cola-bleached version of what everyone perceives as the one and only higher power, but perhaps just a pinch of that endless energy I have been going on about, gently letting me know that sometimes, good things come to those who deserve them.

Loaded up with all my bus possessions, my good friend Geoffrey Elizabeth Head was leading me out of the building and toward the back of the theater where the buses were parked. Every few feet or so I stopped to say good night to everyone along the way—the guys in Papa Roach, the various crew members, the people who worked at the venue, and so forth. The exit was taking a lot longer than the entrance had, but I was smiling and hospitable. Soon we found ourselves in a shadowy part of the stairway, heading down in the direction of the main room and the doors to the outside world. One of the managers of the place graciously put down his rum and Coke and led us out, giving us a hand with our luggage. As he and Geoff walked away, I spun around to take one last look at this historical building that had just spent the night reverberating with our clamor of rock noise. The hall was silent and empty, and I could just see back behind me the stairs I had descended to get to the bottom floor. I looked up.

A shadow ran across the top of the stairs into a different part of the venue, which was closed off. It had moved with incredible speed, and if I had not been paying attention, I would have missed it. It just ran through a door into a completely separate side of the house, as if the door was open and it was totally natural to go in that direction. As quick as it happened, it was over. I stood there in half darkness overwhelmed and gob-smacked. I was all alone in a place that had just let me know I was indeed not alone. Most people at a time like this might do something understandably freakish, like shit their pants or scream like a child actor in his first orgy. These are both very reasonable reactions, and I would applaud anyone for doing so. Me? Yeah, I seem to be a little more fucked up than the average bear because I stood there silently for a full thirty seconds while a huge shit-eating grin spread across my dumb-ass face. A watched pot never boils, you can never make a toaster rush, and a ghost never shows his face until it is dressed for the occasion. In that moment I was very near to being totally sated.

I swung my backpack a little tighter on my back, threw a quiet farewell over my shoulder and flew down the fire escape into the seemingly arctic temperatures of the frozen East Coast evening. I had a chapter for the book after all. I was too happy to be shivering and too tired to give a shit about anything else. I guess the one thing to take from this chapter is perseverance. I could quote a shitty pop song right about now, like Wilson Phillips' "Hold on for One More Day," but you know me. I have just enough asshole in me to respect your notions to give in to a whim like that. Then again, seeing as I just did, suffer and recover, people. If you are not down with the eighties, that is not my problem. You just need to engulf yourself in more sugary junk food music, whether you were alive during that era or not.

I settled onto the bus and looked out the window, still smiling because the weather had chosen to freeze that look on my face until my muscles thawed and allowed me to unclench my jaws. With a laugh, I gave in to temptation and pushed a little appreciation out into the world with one little simple thought of joy. That thought was this: God, I love it here. I love the people, I love the resilience, I love the attitude, and I love the food. I love the generosity that bursts through just when you think it is extinct around these parts. I love the emotion and the sense that everyone around, you are all in this together. I love the fact that no matter what the hell is going on and no matter what hits this place, people get on with life. They get on with living. Whether it is out in the sticks or deep in the city that bears its namesake, whether it is summer, winter, spring, or fall, whether I deserve the charity and the warmth or not . . .

New York, my friend, you never, *ever* let me down.

A FUNNY THING HAPPENED ON THE WAY TO HEAVEN

REMEMBER THE DREAM I told you about in chapter 2? The one in which I am flying around the cavern like Indiana Jones, killing zombies like a boss? And the guy yells at me to take my shoes off? Well, friends and enemies, this one is even stranger. It only happened once, but fuck Moses, it left an impression. Before you ask, no, I am not currently taking any prescription drugs or sniffing Scotchgard. I apparently just have a penchant for fucked up dreams lately. It is times like these when I truly wish there was some kind of headgear or helmet that could capture and record all this weirdness. I think I should have a word with Professor Brian Cox about that, if he ever returns my fan mail. Hopefully he signs my eight-by-ten picture of him too—he is just dreamy . . . sigh . . .

Ahem—sorry.

I came to in my dream doing yard work in my grandmother's yard at her house on the south side of Des Moines. Just popped awake, rake in my hand—no reason for it really. I have not done yard work at my Gram's house in years. So it was a novel sensation, albeit in dream mode. It kind of felt cool to have that old rake in my hand again, plunging it into the leaves furiously. Never mind the fact that there are no trees in my Gram's front yard anymore—we had those cleared years ago. So where the bloody shitter did all these leaves come from? I suppose it is not for me to figure out, just to push into piles so I can jump in.

In my dream it was a typically gray autumn day on the south side. It had that look like it would rain, but there was no moisture in the air. But that was okay because it was a jacket day, and I swear that Des Moines, Iowa, has the best jacket days on the planet. You can wear whatever jacket you want and you will be fine. If you go outside in just a T-shirt, your nipples will cut through corduroy. Put one jacket on, and you are immediately immersed in the Goldilocks Effect: everything is just right.

So there I was, on a perfect jacket day, inexplicably raking leaves that should not have been on my Gram's lawn, when I happened to look up the street.

I saw a lion.

My first reaction was complete nonchalance: "Oh, look at that—another lion." Like it was completely and utterly expected—it is an everyday occurrence to run into the King of the Fucking Jungle on the wild streets of south side Des Moines. Why not? Made sense to me, just as it made sense for the lawn to be loaded with leaves with no trees around. But then again, it *must* have smacked of fantasy, because I turned my attention fully to this beast wandering around the suburbs.

It looked a bit like something you would discover at a Chinese New Year parade, some sort of pantomime lion with short surly gents meandering about, trying their best not to think about the fact that no matter how gruff you pretend to be, you cannot look cool dressed as a lion made of yarn. But as I was contemplating it, something even more fantastic happened. The lion became a horse—not a pantomime horse, but a proper horse. What the hell was going on? It still appeared to have yarn for hair, like a bastard acid trip from a Kroft cartoon—H. R. What-the-fuck. Just as I was getting used to the fact that it had changed from lion to horse, the fucking horse's head opened like a Venus flytrap. Two lidless eyes peered at me down the street. The whole thing had the effect of deleted scenes from *Beetlejuice*. I was horrified, mesmerized, and laughing uncontrollably all at once. I can only compare it to kissing, biting, and shitting your pants simultaneously.

Some time must have passed, because the next thing I know, a Russian woman, who lived across the street from my grandmother the whole time and I did not know about it, was explaining to me how she did not wash her vagina. I bottled off across the street to my house (in real life, I live nowhere near my grandmother) and told my wife about the encounter and about how the Russian woman did not wash her vagina. Her response? "When *does* she?"

That is a true story . . . as far as an imagined nocturnal scenario can be considered true. I might just be using this book as some strange dream journal, now that I think about it. But I guess my point is that nothing is ever what it seems. Just when you think you have everything figured out, the truth will deliver a vicious wallop to your gooch that could tear it open like a trash bag full of prison-house wine, spilling your nut blood for everyone to see. A dose of reality is as healthy as a vitamin every morning but can also be as jarring as a punch in the mouth. No matter how much you shun the inevitable, sometimes you just need to shake your head like a magic eight ball and wait for a different conclusion.

So on that note, let me talk a bit about cryptozoology.

From Bigfoot to Nessie, from the New Jersey Devil to the Wendigo, there has been a place in my heart for this pseudo-science since I saw my first episode of Leonard Nimoy's *In Search Of . . . .* I have learned so much about places like the Bermuda Triangle and the supposed lost civilization of Atlantis from programs that go on little proof but a lot of chutzpah. The show *Ancient Aliens* alone has a special little place in my heart and soul because, according to "ancient astronaut theorists" (the greatest three-word combination ever to be uttered in my presence), almost everything can be traced back to aliens throughout history. You name it, they have a program about how the aliens had a hand in it: Nazis and their various advancements in technology, Aztecs and their advancements in technology, the Bible, angels, Bigfoot, structures that predate man's abilities—I mean, seriously, the lists have become so ridiculous that I watch now just to get a fucking laugh. Now the wonderful thing about these programs is that they start *so* promising. Some of their findings at first do make you stop and go, "Huh, you know, that is quite interesting. Maybe . . ." But then they chime in with the crop circles and the like, and I resign myself to sitting back and enjoying it for what it is—entertainment, with a Hershey bar and some peanut butter. Sherlock Holmes said that one must be careful with assumptions—you run the risk of finding facts to suit theories instead of devising theories to suit facts. That, and you make an "ass" out of "u" and "me," but that in itself is asinine. The world is full of wonderful things without giving all the credit to Ye Olde E.T.

While doing research I uncovered some lovely examples of cryptozoology. Apparently, years ago, people could believe that cotton—patently a plant—was the fruit of something other than vegetation. So a legend grew up around "The Vegetable Lamb of Tartarry." It was believed to be half-plant, half-animal and looked much like a cross between a sheep and a fucking cauliflower. Well, that is at least what the drawings of this being looked like— a sort of artist's representation of a thing that did not exist. But people believed in this strongly because it was during an age when new plants and animals were being discovered all the time. It had been shown that fungi-like mushrooms were a sort of amalgam of flora and fauna, with the visual traits of a plant yet leaning closer to an animal, so at the time it was not that far off the beaten path. Of course, today we know this is nonsense. But think about back then: farmers trying desperately to get their hands on Vegetable Lamb seed and scratching their brains in an effort to figure out what to feed the fuckers when they had flowered. It is very much a bit of Piers Anthony: the land of Xanth would have been loaded with Vegetable Lambs.

I can almost hear your heads shaking, as you say, "Fuck my butter, what does this have to do with anything?" You should know by now that I always have a bit of deviance just around the corner. Give us a second, yeah?

Look, I am not saying there are not some pointless bits of interest out there. It has been going on since before we began letting people like Nicole Richie contribute to the verbal gene pool, coining phrases like "frenemies." I mean, what in the purple fuck is a "biz-cation"? I know it is an amalgam of the words business and vacation, but it is fucking stupid. Also, why would you *ever* have any reason whatsoever for following Wal-Mart or Miracle Whip or fucking Starbucks on Twitter? Why would we follow businesses on a social network? It is the most frivolous and ridiculous bit of nonsense I have ever experienced. Sometimes desperation can be the most nurturing mother of invention, but in this case it smacks of the old guy in the bar trying to pick up the younger girls with liquor and a hot car—it is creepy and it makes me uncomfortable as I look toward the future.

Where the fuck was I?

The reason I bring up cryptozoology is because I want to talk about something that is referred to as "fringe science." In an earlier chapter I discussed reasons why the existence of ghosts could be plausible from a scientific standpoint by explaining how their makeup could be validated using the laws of thermodynamics. This gave me the courage (and terror, to be frank) to put together a bit of calculus based on an idea I call "intelligent energy," which you might remember was S (W + E) × ∞ = ghosts. I am not trying to recreate Maxwell's Equation or anything, but it looks the shit on paper. Well, I am afraid I am about to bombast you with even more science content. So once again, spoiler alert: you may actually learn something in the next few pages.

I can only apologize.

The following bits of fairly relevant data have been pieced together using a few websites and the more credible ends of Wikipedia. I am most annoyingly standing on the shoulders of giants to put these strings of theory together, but give credit where credit is due—I have used pregathered intelligence to reinforce the ideas I am surmising at the moment. Thankfully, this has made my job a little easier. But just so you know: I did my research using preexisting research. It is "all good in the hood," as the kids are prone to say. Then again, the kids also use the acronym YOLO, which means "you only live once," as an excuse to do some of the dumbest shit I have ever had to witness. So maybe I should just stick to the shit I would use, like "fucking get over it." Yeah—that feels more like my style.

Anyway, there is a phenomenon known as an "out-of-body experience." To put it moderately, this is apparently when the spirit leaves the body during death and explores the world around it, even traveling hundreds of miles, but returning to its body upon resuscitation. Doctors refer to this as an NDE, a "near-death experience." It has also been referred to as "astral projection," a popular term coined by the incense addicts. As you might imagine, there is a great deal of research that has arisen that is, to quote the great Stephen Fry, quite interesting.

People have described these extraordinary instances for years. Carl Jung, one of the founding fathers of psychoanalysis, had one himself after a heart attack. As late as 2003 Dr. Peter Lenwick of

London University had found convincing instances of paranormal feats, such as premonitions, telepathy, and, indeed, NDEs. Sharon Cooper and Dr. Kenneth Ring did a similar study in which blind people could see and feel things during an NDE, even if those same people were blind from birth. They were able to describe their surroundings and the goings-on with total accuracy. This coincided with a study done in 2000 by Dr. Bruce Greyson in which "events observed while outside the body were later verified by others." Dr. Karl Jansen, during his research on ketamine, described its effect on a part of the brain known as "the God spot," a version of the archetypal "higher self" or "God Image," which Carl Jung was able to describe after his personal NDE.

The phenomenon has also been called "soul flight." This has to be a phrase created by peyote eaters. I have nothing against imbibers of the Almighty Cactus, but it is stuff like this that leads to strange conversations about who would win in a fight between Bruce Lee and Spiderman. I include it here for one simple reason: I believe there is a correlation between NDEs and the existence of ghosts and spirits. There are some intriguing things that could back up my hypothesis, much like the reasoning I gave on the laws of thermodynamics. Interestingly, some surmise that NDEs correspond to the fringe principles found in quantum physics, such as, and I quote, "properties of light," "multidimensional realities," "the zero-point field," "quantum interconnectivity, consciousness, and synchronicity," "space/time interconnectivity" "time travel" (stick with me, people), "teleportation" (I said stick with me, people!), "nonlocality," "singularities" (i.e., the existence of black holes—any *Star Trek* fan can explain that to you), and "subjectivity."

That is indeed quite a list. I may be fairly confident in my supposition that most of you have a raging fucking brain-ache at the moment. But I refuse to let up on you right now. The gist of this, if it is in fact plausible, is that if these various laws and theorems can establish reasonable evidence to support NDEs, the same can be done for ghosts and spirits. You might think, "surely, this cannot be the case," and you may be right—most scientists regard this "evidence" as fairly pompous work, or garbage science. In a lot of ways this casts a fairly puritanical shadow on that specific side of the researching society in general, for supposedly a scientist's first response should always be "we do not know yet" and not "that is not plausible" until it has been exhaustively scrutinized. The latter is the outburst of the religious, who believe all their answers can be found in ancient texts instead of in the world around them. I would like to think that the many communities of studious peoples might some day regard this with more query than scoffing.

If we could get back to the list of examples that caused everyone to run screaming for the aspirin, I will continue.

Let's look at the properties of light—more importantly, electromagnetic radiation, or EMR. This is a form of energy that is emitted and absorbed by charged particles. Electromagnetic radiation carries radiant energy through space, continuously away from its source. To me, that means that energy can exist autonomously from the body's source. So in NDEs many scientists conjecture that the will and soul may be able to exist away from the physical body during temporary death. Why might this not support my "intelligent energy" idea? If we can accept that a soul can live away from the body when it is temporarily dead, what about during a more permanent state of death? There seems to be evidence that energy can coalesce spontaneously. What is to say that a soul, broken from its physical self, may not establish itself when the source is gone? It may be a stretch, but to me it makes perfect sense. Then again, I have been known to talk out of various stinky orifices.

M-theory deals with multidimensional realities, which is an extension of string theory. Before you burn this book in protest, let me get to the point on this example: it deals with low-entropy content. For those who do not know, entropy explains that in nature all systems are breaking down. It is one of the reasons why perpetual-motion machines will never work on this plane of existence. So low-entropy content involves cycles that fade much more slowly than others. I include it here because in my intelligent energy idea, it may explain why some ghosts are more cognizant than others are. Even though matter and energy do not break down, the sentient thought may erode. Also, because string theory deals with the eleven dimensions that have been identified, maybe these spirits can transgress the membranes of these dimensions.

Please tell me you are not bored right now. This is fascinating stuff, really. I have never committed the time to looking for answers like this. I know this chapter may have many of you wishing death on me, but this explanation is necessary. For the skeptics this very well may be reasonable doubt. For the believers like myself, it is a valid exercise so we can all say, "Maybe we are not all crazy!" Unfortunately, for the zealots it may give them ammo for the whole heaven thing. But I take my chances and push on. Now the scientific folk may just turn around and dismiss this because I have not based any of this on my own research; I have merely stood on tiptoes and grabbed other people's jelly on the higher shelves. Fair enough. That is of course a valid point. But the eternal bastard in me may just reverse the poles on that and say it does not mean I am wrong, just lazy.

Moving on!

A zero-point energy field is the minimum energy a quantum mechanical system may have. This means the body can coalesce even with the most slender bit of energy to draw from. So in a zero-point energy field, it *could* be possible for a ghost to manifest by drawing from the heat in the air, the electricity of any mechanical machinery close by, or even any heat that a live person's body gives off. We talked about batteries being drained and going dead just prior to paranormal activity. This would mean that the spirit could borrow energy from any number of places. In the Mansion in California, the thermostat was constantly jumping up, until it was unbearably hot. Could this be because the spirits were encouraging the temperature in order to draw that very heat and materialize? It is an interesting concept—this would mean that it knew how to amp up its own manifestation, which would suggest intelligent thought. Of course, it could mean that the thermo was rubbish and I am an asshole of the highest caliber. This is *all* guesswork, mind you—I have no doctorates, no diplomas, no documentation to suggest my ideas have any basis in reality. I am smarter than the average bear and loaded with imagination—nothing more. But in a sense it does make sense.

This is where it gets tricky, because some of the following theories are not widely accepted. Truly, during my research, a lot of this data carried a disclaimer that some of these ideas required a sort of ratification or endorsement. This was true even on Wikipedia, where anyone and their fucking mom can change information regularly. On Wikipedia, people have changed my own page several times erroneously, making my middle name

Josh and saying I had done extensive work with Tech Nine, both of which are not true. It is a website I tend to avoid like a gnarly dose of syphilis, but I found myself on it just doing backup work. So if even Wikipedia is not sure whether or not the following ideas are okay to list, a written caution by myself would almost be a requisite. So you have been warned: some of these ideas are nefarious in nature . . . and Wikipedia is fucking bullshit.

Quantum interconnectivity deals with quantum entanglement, which is a form of quantum superposition, or duality. It reads, "a measurement is made and it causes one member of such a pair to take on a definite value." It goes on to say that "the other member of this entangled pair will be found to have taken on the appropriately correlated value in a mirror-image action." This is apparently limited to the speeds of normal space-time. But this is where the debate flares up. The argument is whether or not "a classical underlying mechanism could explain why this correlation occurs instantaneously even when the separation distance is large." In other words, in this scenario, suppose the mirror-image action is the body and the spirit divorced from one another. Would both have sentient thought? If we just looked at this from the point of view of the NDE, how far can a soul be from its body and still thrive? If we are to take it on face value, this is not possible. And yet we see example after example of just the opposite. In my own experience even those who refuse to take it seriously have described flying during dreams and astral projection. This is not contrary evidence; this is just expounding on my part. This idea raises more questions than answers, so it is just an example of how these spirits *might* exist.

If you thought that was strange, you are going to love this.

Quantum consciousness deals with the quantum mind. It is a hypothesis proposing that classical mechanics cannot explain human consciousness. I mean let's be honest: consciousness is still a mystery, even after years of study. We have mapped the brain extensively, but there are still no reasons why "we think, therefore we are." We are walking, talking miracles of undisclosed information. People go on and on, waxing poetically about the human plights of sentient thought, but there are no facts about the soul and willpower—only really good guesses. Incidentally, when I was doing my research, I tried to find some scientific studies about willpower. The only articles that popped up were seminars on how to be a more positive thinker in the workplace . . . and, of course, how to quit smoking. So this is me putting together some ideas on how willpower may influence things like energy and the human soul. Quantum mechanical phenomena like entanglement and superposition may play an important role in the brain's function and might someday form the basis of an explanation of consciousness, but at this moment, when we are capable of seeing the light from galaxies that emanated before this planet was even created and is only now reaching us, there are still so many mysteries here in the confines of our own souls.

Quantum synchronicity is a bit of fiddly work. The reason I bring it up here is because I believe it could explain why *both* sides of this debate may be right. In other words, my chances of being on target are just as good as the folks with the white coats and the PhDs. This is summed up in the EPR paradox, written by Albert Einstein, Boris Podolsky, and Nathan Rosen—the aforementioned EPR, respectively. My ideas may be supported by this paradox, specifically the second half, which says that information—or, in this case, proof—may be encoded in "hidden parameters." They were trying to debunk another piece of quantum physics and in doing so, basically came up with the idea that just because you have not found the answers, that does not mean the answers are not there. At least that is the way I read it. I happily look forward to your letters of disgust.

Here is a last little bit of my examples of plausibility: gravitational singularity, or space-time singularity. This is "a location where the quantities that are used to measure the gravitational field become infinite in a way that does not depend on the coordinate system." To me, that may mean that the spirits in question, according to my intelligent energy idea, may be able to sustain themselves by borrowing from different sources of power. Gravitational singularity deals with the curvatures of space-time and includes a measure of the density of matter. Only in the last few years have we realized that the darkness of space—the black shit we see surrounding the stars at night—is matter, not just emptiness. So the idea is that everything has matter, even on a macrolevel, and if everything has matter, that means everything (and I do mean *everything*) has the potential to produce energy.

So, based on that last paragraph, let me break this shit down like a hardcore band for you. The spirit (a location where the quantities are measured in the gravitational field) can separate from the body (the coordinate system that the location does not need to depend on) and sustain itself through other sources of energy, which I surmise from *all* of the information I have spewed on the corresponding pages. If the last century has showed me anything, it is that anything is possible. From governing dynamics to thermodynamics, the only basis to support a negative retort to the idea of intelligent energy—or ghosts—is skeptical narcissism. Those who have higher degrees of education are pedantic enough to argue these points until they are blue in the face, and yet there are so many things that can support the idea, and that is *all* this is—an idea. I am not bucking for a Nobel Prize or even an Ignoble Prize; I am merely trying to make sense of the things I have seen and experienced in the best way I know how—through the many trains of fact and supposition that science has afforded us over the millennia. Even Einstein was not taken seriously when he first theorized that space was curved; it was not until pictures were carefully taken of a solar eclipse that he was proven right. But he knew it all along. Remember: the answers may indeed be in those "hidden parameters."

I refuse to revert to myth or other tales of the past that tried to explain these things according to tired examples of imagination. I will never subscribe to a method of immediate dismissal, because that is what so many nonbelievers have done based solely on the fact that it does not make sense *to them*. How can so many people talk about basically the same things and yet still have so many intellects treat these ideas as detritus? How can so many people have the gift of knowledge and not see there may be something there? When imagination and intellect graft themselves together, we find ourselves swimming in possibility, not detriment. If this were the case, people would have never pushed through the veils of prospect to the land of discovery. We would have virtually none of the many wonderful advancements we have today, from pasteurization to space travel. Someone had to go first. Someone had to leave the pack of nay-saying bastards and take the faltering steps toward the unknown. I am in no way saying that person is me—I am just a messenger. But my role is to present possible ideas, not semantics and bullshit. The status quo is not always right, and that, to me, is a relief. If it were, the world would be worse because of it.

Did you know that when a person dies, they are twenty-one grams lighter than when they were alive? This disrupts the whole idea of "dead weight," quite frankly. Dead weight only means the difficulty of carrying a dead body because the body in question cannot get involved, making it hard to coordinate. And god knows I have carried my share of dead bodies—er, I mean, god knows I have watched several movies in which carrying a dead body looks like it would be uncomfortable and watching said movie in no way means I engaged in any unsavory or illegal behavior and can also account for whereabouts on any given night in question, officer. I have no idea where I was at this point in the conversation . . . something about a movie . . . wait, Sean Penn . . . Benicio Del Toro . . . OH YEAH!! *21 Grams*—awesome flick, you should see it. And before you ask, yes, I am feeling much better now.

The twenty-one grams idea has been tested, and it seems to be true. This suggests that the human soul has mass. We already know that the soul is energy. Now we know it has mass. As I said before and as scientific discovery has told us, mass and energy *do not break down*. They do not go away. So the human soul cannot go away. Seeing as I do not believe in heaven, there are so many plausible instances and scenarios available if you put your mind to it. The energy could be distributed to other systems. The spirit could be recycled into another life form, vis-à-vis reincarnation, which is probable when you put it in context. But by that notion, applying these ideas to the same examples, it is indeed possible for a spirit to exist when it is broken from its host.

So the question now becomes: what *kind* of energy is it?

Yeah, at this point I am just showing off. Plus I am fairly certain I just triggered thousands of new headaches. I hate to think I am making any of you think. But then again, if you do not think, how else are you going to learn? My Board of Education has holes drilled in it and leaves a vicious wound. In other words, the truth might hurt, but facts only sting, so bite down and bear with me.

Maxwell's Equation, which I mentioned earlier, deals with commonality between the three major sources of electromagnetic fields: light, magnetism, and electricity. All three travel at the speed of light, which is approximately 186,000 miles per second. These are the Big Three, our major sources of energy. What if the human spirit was a fourth? It is an intriguing idea that unfortunately raises more questions than it answers. I will delightfully give you a respite from all this hogwash for a while.

Here is a great way to change it up: Ouija boards are fucking horseshit.

I cannot tell you how many exasperating arguments I have had with people over the relevance and demonstrative features of these pieces of hokum from Parker Brothers. It was not even originally designed for contact with the dead: it was supposed to be an artistic form of automatic writing, a way to contact your "self." But ever since movies like *The Exorcist* and *Witchboard,* Goths and nutbags everywhere carry these things into graveyards and abandoned buildings to "talk to the other side," like these boards are some type of MagicJack Plus subscription or something. What happens when the dead reverse the charges, I wonder?

It does not get much more beyond the fringe than a fucking Ouija board, and it does not take much more effort to fuck with people than to participate maliciously in a ceremony in which one such board is involved. I have never given them much thought—to me, they are no different than cold readers, tarot cards, and divining the future through tea leaves—the soft-core porn of the astrology sects. But nevertheless people are convinced the Ouija board is a broadband CB radio to the afterlife.

They have used them for contacting everyone from Houdini to Elvis. Some friends invited me to one of the things—they called it a séance, which is a nice way to dress up a bullshit session or a meeting of vapid minds. So I begrudgingly acquiesced. But I had silly high jinks in mind.

We sat in an old house just outside Denver, off of a road that leads you up to Red Rocks Amphitheater. I think my friend Jester was there, but I may be mistaken. All I know is that I was a million miles from reason and up to no good. I do remember there was a woman who called herself Rose there. Her real name was, like, Ingrid or something, so good call on the pseudonym. But with that name came all the haughty trimmings of a pretentious Thanksgiving. It was her Ouija board, and she had tried to dirty it up, or "antique it" as they say, by writing on it and scuffing it presumably with dirt. The only problem was that she kept it in the original box—the fucking thing still had the price tag from Wal-Mart on it. That was not going to rain on her dramatic parade though. "Ooooh, derelict spirits!" she exclaimed in the din, startling me and nearly making me wee a little. "We seek your guidance, wisdom, and cherished mercy . . . SPEAK THROUGH ME. Speak to us. Speak to . . . the world!"

You got to be fucking kidding.

And so the circling began. There we were: a bunch of gothic punk nightmares, fingers all together and touching on a piece of plastic with a hole in it, watching it swirl around like none of us had anything to do with its movement. I know for a fact that I was pushing it; I had no illusions coming into the damn thing. Then again, I had nefarious intentions. Slowly but surely, I started to lead this plastic triangle toward the letters that I wanted. I started with a Y, then an O, until I made it spell out a single sentence:

"YOU ARE ALL IDIOTS."

I had planned on making it say, "YOU ARE ALL GONNA DIE," but I changed it at the last minute because I did not want to run the risk of stepping in someone's piss after scaring three shades of shit out of a group composed of armchair vampires—and I use the term "vampire" here as loosely as possible. Rose, being a little savvier than I gave her credit, picked up on it before I was done and scowled at me the rest of the night. She then called an end to the séance. I was not invited back. As you can tell, my feelings are still hurt to this day. I had basically pulled this same prank on some of my friends back in Evansdale, Iowa, when I carved a Ouija board face onto the top of a writing plank. Guiding the makeshift stylus, which was nothing more than the bottom of a Pepsi two-liter bottle, I made my board tell them all to bum me cigarettes. They all complied. I had smokes for the rest of the night. We did this for a few weeks every Saturday, about an hour before *Headbangers Ball* came on MTV. Good times. Good friends. Good smokes.

So yeah—those games are shite.

The wonderful thing about all this science and math I am hitting you with is that I am so very fallible when it comes to these questions. Everything I wrote may not even make fucking sense at the end of the day. A theorist could read this book and treat it like the *National Enquirer*. I could become a punch line for the entire scientific world, a Munson among men. But who gives a shit? So maybe I have just committed the worst bit of mental clutter since Garth Brooks tried to make a rock album, or at least since Chris Cornell tried to make a hip-hop album, or at least since Scott Weiland tried to make a Christmas album, or at least since Lil Wayne tried to make a metal album (I could do this all day—you get the picture . . .). Maybe this is the biggest put-on since the Millerites experienced their Great Disappointment in 1844. But ladies and gentlemen of the jury . . . what if I am not crazy? What if in some corner of a college basement somewhere someone could take this numeral voodoo and actually *get* somewhere with it? All I have done is stand on a step stool with a lit book of matches, doing my best to set the sprinklers off and send the alarms howling.

Discovery is a violent spasm of chance, reason, and determination. It takes a bit of ball size to jump in among the fires and dare for a marriage of the factual and the fascinating. In this day and age, when everything we are surrounded by seems to be less and less positive, when the world always finds itself on the dagger's edge, just waiting for the final showdown, and even religion, with all its bells and whistles, cannot drag the throng away from wishing it was a quicker end than slower agony, maybe, just maybe, these few pages can be a counterweight to the heaviness life and all its trimmings can bring. What is so bad about not only believing in ghosts but also in trying to supply a few mathematical examples of why it is possible? What is the matter with wanting just a little bit of mystery left in the world, out there on the fringe by the Yetis and the underwater civilizations? This reality can and will kick every inch of fuck right out of you if you give it an ample opening. We have the anchor—how about a little wind in our sails?

I think looking backward is not the answer, as many theologians would want us to do. I also taste a little tactical chowder when I hear a pragmatist flailing at the mouth about how things like spirits cannot and never did exist. The bile in their repudiations causes the muscles in my forearms to draw clenched fists together and play a game I like to call Smash the Weasel. I only relax when I consider the hypocrisy of it all, when I have the same reaction to the God Squad. So the Gentleman Scholar inside me soothes my troubled mind and furrowed brow with the subtle yet firm reminder that "maybe time will tell . . ." Souls are wonderful things that no one can explain. We do know that this fleshy vessel we use for digs gives off a shit ton of energy. There has to be a connection. There has to be a little triple fantastic in this. Otherwise, humanity as a whole would not be so wonderfully and gloriously fucked up and beautiful.

In this chapter I picture myself running around a giant stone laboratory with crazy tall white hair and a toothy grin, pouring smoking noxious potions from one beaker to another, twisting knobs and switching switches, making lots of noise and cackling like a madman. My gnarled and hunched assistant wanders behind me (I call him Skip because I never bothered to stop and learn his real name), waiting to do my bidding while he wrings his hands over and over, as if there is too much lotion on them. In a convulsion of triumph, I savor my "eureka" moment with rigorous vigor and run across the stones to a blackboard covered in pagan-like symbols and chalk dust. With a bellow of "AH-HA!" I launch myself into my work again, muttering, "I will show them all! I will show the world! I will have my revenge!" Then again, I picture myself like that a lot, really. I see myself like that when I am making lunch sometimes. So I guess this new vision is nothing new. But I like it. I should look into buying a castle with a dungeon somewhere.

The point is that stranger things are always possible. We keep finding mysteries and unlocking their answers, more so in the last twenty years than at any other time in our existence, in my opinion. Yes, things like alchemy and perpetual-motion machines are a little outside our grasp of physics, but there are vast universes of explorative discovery to be had if only we have the mettle to make it so. Just because something is fantastic does not mean it is a fantasy that will never find its place in reality. One of the better bits of being human is that we can dream and reach for things that might never have been reached if we had not had the power to do the dreaming in the first place. The only limits we have ever had are the ones we build ourselves, fences of pessimistic stone that keep out the sun while blinding us to the sensation of that light on our faces. Some claim that only God has the answers; others say that the parameters of science section off the places we are not meant to go. All of that could be true. Then again, all of that could be a crutch to ensure that the majority of humanity remains ignorant and shortsighted. How will we ever find ourselves if we are not allowed to look? How will we outlast the mistakes of the past unless we test the waters outside our peripheral vision?

Maybe ghosts do not exist. Maybe there is no way in science and life that they can exist. Maybe I have more mental instability than I thought. Maybe I am wrong. If I am, then I will be the first to admit it. I would not like the taste of saying it and I would grumble into my coffee cup for a few years, but I would accept it and move on to the next mystery. Maybe I just have a great propensity for turning bullshit into brilliance than do most people I know. But I like my idea better—that there is more to this world and others than even we, with our big brains and brawny opinions, can fathom as of yet. I like thinking that somewhere between the religion and the science there is the truth. We may never know. But that does not mean that we will never dream of its identity.

THE KIDS
ON THE
CIRCLE

I N 2006 I FOUND MYSELF IN a very strange dichotomy. On the professional side, everything was going swimmingly. Stone Sour had just released *Come What(ever) May,* we had just come off a great run on the Family Values tour, and "Through Glass" was number one on the radio, on its way to staying there for eleven weeks. I had been working and touring for seven years by that point, and even though I knew there was more work ahead, I felt like I had a good foothold in the zeitgeist, cementing myself in the industry and setting the foundation for a thrillingly long career. I had also sold millions of albums, played several sold-out shows, and won a Grammy award with Slipknot. I was really hitting my stride, both musically and intellectually, and I was ready for anything.

Unfortunately my flipside was desperate to know how the other half lived. I was separated, on my way to an eventual divorce, and sleeping in my friends' basement on a pullout couch that had seen a few too many doggy naps. I would not quite call it the glamorous life, but suffice it to say I was happy and that was what mattered. It was the beginning of that long road I have described in other literary routes as "getting it together, for fuck's sake." Although my friends had made it very clear that I could stay as long as I wanted, I knew I would need to get off my ass and find myself a home—that is what you do: you get your shit together, mend, and move on. Life only does you favors when you show the world you have the legs for a journey like that. So in late 2006, with my friends' help, I went house hunting again. Unlike last time, I was not exactly looking for anything monumental or manor-like. I just wanted something that I could move into very quickly—comfortable, durable, cozy, and suitable for soirees and a few parties here and there. But every available house I looked at just did not have that thing I was looking for. I know what you are thinking: does something like that matter? Well, to me, yes, something like that does matter. Emotionally speaking, I had just moved out of Alaska. I wanted a home in the spiritual tropics.

At a friend's urging I went back to one of the many houses I had originally turned down that I was convinced needed too much work. Like I said before, I wanted something ready-made and did not want to waste any time on shit like picking out curtains to match the carpets or any shit like that. I wanted this transition to be efficient and speedy. So I had no real expectations when I found myself walking through a certain two-story split-level in my hometown that day. But once I realized a little TLC would make it perfect (and some assurances that this could be done while I was on the road because I am a lazy cunt when it all comes down to it), I went for the little house on the cul-de-sac on the west side of my beloved Des Moines. Despite the work that needed to be done to my future home, I had high hopes and was dealing with an excitement I had not felt in my life. This was the big time—a house of my own. No roommates, no people to trash the place, no bullshit—just my son and I when it was my time to have him. Over the course of a month spent off the road, I slowly moved my stuff in while augmenting with things I was in dire need of, like couches, tables . . . and a fifty-five-inch big-screen TV with 7.1 surround sound.

You know—necessities . . .

After the renovations were completed, the house was wonderfully affable. We had removed a wall on the first floor and opened the living room and kitchen into one great big entertaining area. Up had come some dreary tile and carpet; down had gone some kick-ass hardwood flooring in its place. The formal dining room was a particular favorite. The wood floors were stolen from a house I had looked at twice, had made offers on, and had been about to close on when the owner had freaked out, taking the house off the market completely. The last I heard, the agent involved was suing the guy. But there had been a great floor plan in which several kinds of wood had been used in a remarkable way that really made the floor pop. So seeing as I had not been able to get the actual house, I just stole the idea for its most striking feature. Anyway, the rest of my house was painted and prepped (including some granite counters in the kitchen, called "Uba Tuba"), and after a few months it was finally finished.

I was ready to get on with my life in a house that I could call my own and around which I could build on my family. It had a great backyard, nice neighbors, and enough privacy that I did not need to hire armed security to man the parapets, so to speak. Sure, I was gone on the road a lot, but everyone and their mom loved the place, and my son made fast friends with the children living next door, running the area like I had when I was growing up. Contrary to the plans I had made when I first purchased the house, I soon had a few roommates too. They filled a vacancy for looking after the place when I was gone and provided company when I was resting from the burdens of touring and travel. But the first night I stayed there I was by myself, and it became very apparent that once again, in a very different house on a very different side of town, I was not living alone, not by a fucking long shot.

That first night I was lying in bed on my way to sleep. There was no one else in the house; my son was not with me that night, and I had no guests staying at the time. But just as I was drifting away, I clearly heard footsteps running across the hardwoods on the first floor. At first I was sure I was dreaming. There was no way this house could have spirits, and the chances that I had found *another* haunted house after the fiasco on Foster Drive were as remote as the Chicago Cubs winning back-to-back World Series titles. I mean, the house itself was built in the mid-eighties, and the neighborhood was practically a baby: when I was a teenager, this area was nothing more than a flicker of life in a land developer's lonely penis; the only thing for miles had been a Casey's General Store, where I had occasionally gone to steal, I mean, "buy" cigarettes. I just could not allow myself to think that this had anything to do with the paranormal. So I listened again for a second and let it go, sure that I had imagined it.

Then it happened again, but this time louder.

I shot up in bed and made ready to investigate. I was still certain there was no otherworldly connection. What I was not sure about was if I had remembered to lock all the doors. Just for a little background here, around this time there was a criminal in the area known only as "the WDM Rapist" stalking the "mean" West Des Moines streets and assaulting women. Not knowing his modus operandi, I was not going to take a chance that someone was not wandering around my new home up to no good. I grabbed my Louisville Slugger nicknamed "The Widow Maker" and began a steady descent to the first floor. I checked every nook and cranny, pretending I knew something about police procedure for clearing corners in unexplored rooms, but really I just watch too much *Law and Order: SVU.* I got to my kitchen at the heart of the house and leaned against the "Uba Tuba" countertop (sorry—I just love saying "Uba Tuba") on the cooking island at its center, nudging myself for being a tool bag. I was turning toward the hallway to the stairs when I clearly heard the running behind me, coming up fast. I flew around, high on adrenaline. Of course, when your imagination is fueled by that much crazy gasoline, there is nothing that will really surprise you. So I was at least expecting to see some dumpy, hairy douche bag, dressed all in black with a woolly balaclava pulled over his greasy hair in an attempt to be incognito. When I found no one there, the shock was almost too much to bear.

And so that is how it has gone for the entire time I have lived here. It happens while I am home. It happens while I am gone. It happens whether my son is here or not. It has continued to happen after I met The Boss. She eventually moved in, and we have made it our home together, even before we were married. It always seems to happen when we just space it off and forget about it, as though the spirits who play chaos with the house do not really want to show themselves too often, but they lose their minds if we seem like we are ignoring them. At times we have been sitting on the couch watching TV with friends and family alike, completely undisturbed, and we all abruptly hear running in the upstairs bedrooms. But you have to love the resignation of the previously initiated. Being used to it, my wife and I just yell, "KNOCK IT OFF UP THERE!" and go back to watching our program. Our guests, however, go ashen and look at us like we are crazy. Our response is always the same: "What, you have never yelled at children before?"

Yes, our extraspecial housemates are indeed children. We know that for a few reasons: one, my wife and I have seen them with our own eyes; two, we can hear them laughing while they play, and they almost always play in either my son's room or the spare bedroom next to it; three, they mock people's speech in tiny voices; and four, they fuck with people in very childlike ways. Trust me: I will get to all the stories in a second. But let me council you against freaking out like some people who have stayed at or lived in my house. They are also very harmless. Sure, they are mischievous and do things that drive me crazy sometimes. But there is nothing malevolent about these children. If there was, we would not still live here. With the exception of a few physical confrontations, the kids on the circle have really just been extra children fucking around in this midwestern suburban household. However, I do not care how tough you are—ghost children can be exceedingly creepy.

I was upstairs in the master bathroom taking a shower one day. Griffin had a friend over and was playing somewhere loudly, as you will have with kids his age. I was not too worried about his whereabouts because there were people downstairs having lunch who could keep an eye on the young wrecking crew. I excused myself to bathe because I came to the startling conclusion that I smelled like the groin of a bull dipped in poop. I decided to do something about that, so I bathed and was just drying off as I stepped into the outer part of the bathroom. There are double doors that open into the bedroom; if you go out of those doors and turn to the right, you will see the bed and the door to the upstairs hallway and the stairs that lead you down to the living room and so on. There is not a lot of room to play, so as I looked up and saw children in the bedroom, streaking by the doors, I thought little of it. I was wearing a towel, and it was a quick dash to get out of the room, which was the direction they were heading. I stepped into the bedroom, thinking I would see the kids. They were nowhere around. I threw on some pants and ran down to chastise my son and his friends for playing in there while I was taking a shower. But my friends let me know they were all outside—in fact, they had not been inside the whole time I was up there. I stood there, knowing I had chased children out of the room. In that moment I knew they were not the kids I had thought they were.

As I have said, stuff like this happens all the time. It is especially annoying when it happens in the morning, when I am busy getting Griffin up for school while simultaneously trying to prepare his breakfast and school lunch, functioning on little or no sleep. There have been mornings when I have been standing in my kitchen, waiting for my blessed coffee to brew, and suddenly I hear little footsteps running up from behind. I turn around, expecting to see Griff, bright eyed and bushy tailed, ready for school. Instead I am presented with an empty kitchen. One time I was making my son some Pop-Tarts while also cooking something in the microwave. My back was to the counter closest to the sink, and he had not made it downstairs yet. So imagine my surprise when an invisible presence sent Griffin's aluminum thermos flying across that same countertop, landing with a loud "CLANK" in the sink. It scared me so badly that I had to check my pajama bottoms for brown Bingo dots. Note to ghosts: please refrain from this sort of mischief before I have had my morning java. Sometimes they just run about, which makes sense, seeing as the floor plan is wide open and made for games of tag. Other times they can be so damn confounding, like hiding Griffin's lunch bag in a place so remote that I end up sending him to school with a brown bag full of food. Then the next day it magically appears again. I do not have time to go on some scavenger hunt sent from the other side for stuff that I bought in the first fucking place.

Griffin is no stranger to these unseen high jinks as well. There was an instance a while back that happened during a period when his Aunt Christine was watching him. She had just gotten him up for school and was enjoying the ritual of it all. They were sitting at the kitchen table during breakfast, joshing with each other and poking fun like kids and adults are prone to do—pushing buttons playfully and giggling like crazy people. Griff was mimicking Christine, and she was doing likewise, eventually turning the situation into a whole lot of "meh meh MEH meh meh," using a sort of baby voice and crinkling their faces at each other. They were the only ones in the house.

From the formal living room, halfway across the house, a tiny voice said, "Meh meh MEH meh meh."

According to Christine, she went ashen. Griffin immediately asked, "What was that?" She played it off like it was an echo of some kind or a noise from outside. As soon as she got home from taking him to school, though, she frantically called a friend to come over and hang out with her because she did not want to be in the house by herself for a while. Now, she did not feel threatened or anything; it was just a little unsettling. And rightly so: had I been in the same situation, I would have done the same thing—not because I felt danger but because that shit just makes your fucking skin crawl. I get that feeling when I am alone in the house, on the couch watching TV, and suddenly someone runs across the kitchen and up behind me. It is disturbing. It also pisses me off. Thank god for DVR so I can rewind what I missed while I was busy pissing myself.

Oh fuck yeah, that is another thing—they end up creating a lot of goddamn housework for the rest of the troupe and me. Sometimes it is casual little stuff like showing off the ability to move things, and other times I damn near have to call FEMA to come in and help me with the recovery process. The shit is annoying at times and excruciating at others. For instance, I was in the basement with a friend playing *Tiger Woods Golf* (if I hear *one* person judge me . . .) when we heard a monstrous crash come from the Vault. Upon inspection, the little shits had knocked an entire row of my DVDs off of a shelf and onto the floor. It took me a half hour to get them back up and alphabetized. We returned to the game . . . only to have it happen again minutes later. I gave up and left them on the floor for days. It seems like they love to fuck with us while we are in the basement. They turn the lights on and off. They close doors. They run up the stairs. My friend Asian Robby stopped going into the basement entirely after all three of these events happened one night while he was down there spending "quality time" with a special lady friend. I do not feel bad for him; serves him right for hooking up on my couch without asking—or at least without providing video. Besides, it leaves him more time to spend on his hair.

Roy Mayorga was crashing in my basement one time while we were having rehearsals during the making of *Audio Secrecy*. I had offered him the guest bedroom, but he said he was fine with the couch in the basement. Besides, the basement had the fifty-five-inch TV with surround sound, so I could see the appeal. He woke up the next day with scratches all over his neck. Next to him, lying on the floor, was a tiny toy gun made for an action figure, with skin sticking on the end of it. We were all so freaked out we took pictures of it. But upon inspection, we realized that the scratches were actually a heart—they had carved a little heart on his neck, perhaps as a sign of affection. Even so, Roy had a hard time crashing at my house after that—so much for making friends through chivalry and acts of kindness. Then again, I cannot say that I blame him. After being pushed down the stairs by an invisible assailant in the Foster house, if tiny hands wielding G.I. Joe props assaulted me, even with love on their minds, I would probably bail and get a hotel room myself.

The "Kids" on the Circle have a habit of running from room to room like psychotic sugar junkies, as I have mentioned before. One time some friends stopped by the house to see if we were home. We were out running errands, but the upstairs lights were on, giving the appearance that we were indeed home. From the vantage point of the two windows by the front door, you can see the stairs leading to the second floor and the top of the stairs, but then your view is cut off, and if you do see someone, you only see their feet. Our friends were fairly freaked out when they saw three sets of tiny legs running through the hallway at the top of the stairs clad in dresses, black pants, and shiny dress shoes, especially after they learned we were not even home at the time. When they described the shoes, I knew they were our "other" children: I had seen and heard them in all my encounters over the years. Those shoes are not distinct, but the noises they make are for sure—that clackety-clack of hard soles on hardwood is definitely hard to forget.

I wish I could say that the nonsense stops there, but the Kids do shit like that all the time. There was an instance when they knocked the books off of Griff's shelves while he was at his mother's house. It was really no big deal because it had happened before, but for some reason I was in a mood and did not feel like picking up all those damn books. So I tried to beat the system: we decided to lean his bookshelf on the floor so instead of standing up, it was lying on its side. I then shoved the books back on it at an angle, so if they were pushed off, it did not matter seeing as they were literally centimeters from being on the floor to begin with. Yeah, I felt pretty proud—I had successfully outwitted invisible miscreants no older than my son. Go ahead and crown me a genius on the same wavelength as Isaac Newton and Alexander Pope. I was confident nothing could happen after that. So imagine my chagrin when I walked into Griffin's room and all of his books—and I do mean *all* of them—were stacked up in the middle of his room, one on top of the other, creating some sort of Leaning Tower of Books. It was crazy and cool and totally defiant. I deflated. I actually left them like that for a whole day out of spite, just because I knew I would have to put them away in the end. After that I just went back to the regular schedule of cleaning up after them—it was less pride lost on my part.

They change the channels on the TV in the living room, so when you wake up, it is always on Nickelodeon or Disney. You know how unsettling it is to turn on the telly, expecting to see ESPN, and you get *Dora the Explorer,* set at a deafening volume? That triggered my only really angry outburst at them. I just let out a loud "Oh, COME ON!" and scared the absolute fuck out of myself in the process. It was in that moment of pure humanity that I realized the absurdity of that exclamation: a grown man in the wee hours of the morning, yelling at things in his house he would never be able to explain to normal folks, because they had inconveniently changed the channel on him, therefore causing him to have to physically pick up the remote control and put it back on the channel he had been hoping for in the first place. I have to be honest: I really felt like a Craftsman's tool bag in that space and time. But those innocent little fuckers are not as innocent as my wife would lead you to believe. They also constantly "terrorize" anyone who stays at the house by him or herself. Our friend Lady watched our house for a while and would report running in the kitchen while her back was turned and things being knocked over in the office at the end of the house when no one else was with her. As she detailed it, she would sit resigned on the couch, close her eyes, and say aloud, "Oh good . . ." That statement alone was enough to give me fits. Remember, this is the same Lady we do everything in our power to scare on a daily basis because when she panics, it is hysterical. So I cannot fault the Kids for trying to have a little fun at her expense.

Of course, The Boss never lets this shit faze her. She just shrugs her shoulders and says, "They are kids—what the fuck do you expect them to do?"

I swear I would expect nothing less from that woman. The Boss has a way of seeing these things move through our reality that is truly amazing. She can always feel when something is going to happen. She has an uncanny way about her of just knowing, but not just knowing. She can see several solutions to any scenario within seconds of that scenario playing itself out. In other words, she understands things easier and can then relate them back to you in a way that your mind can comprehend. It was through her that I really developed the idea that these things, no matter how strange or physical, are not to be feared. They are intriguing and mysterious, yes, but I will not fear them because they only really want our attention. They are not trying to organize a union and take over the world. You would think I would have every reason to, after being pushed down stairs and seeing my friends get carved on with tiny plastic weapons, but I do not fear these phenomena. They are like involuntary spasms with the rare case of clarity. We must learn from these experiences as much as we can if we are to understand them and add them to our pantheon of realms and reason. In this, I acquiesce to my wife. I realized long ago that she is exceedingly right on a regular basis; I do my best to just keep up.

My wife was the one who first acknowledged that maybe these kids were from the old house on Foster. I had not even been sure that there *were* kids in the old manor house, but then again, the Shadow Man had routinely dominated all of that activity, taking my focus off of anything else that had really been there. The Boss seemed pretty confident that they had most likely arrived with the majority of the stuff I had kept from the old place. So that brings me to another fit of thought: do spirits tie themselves to one place forever or can they move about? Is it their will that allows them to stay or go, or is it the little electrons that get superattracted and cling to one place or person, unconsciously drawing on the magnetism inherent in its being? Think of the concept of soul mates. Certain people are just simply drawn to one another, for better or worse and whether that coupling leads to anything positive or negative. I have seen and felt this sensation myself; I know this to be true. Why does this happen? Maybe our souls are made of a wholly different type of energy that can cause a physical reaction and instant connection when they are near a similar soul they are enamored with or they find something wonderful in common with. If this were true, it could explain a few things in this world and the next.

My wife also posited that maybe this was the case. Maybe there was something about my soul and my personality that made them feel safe. Being around something as fucked up as the Shadow Man, I could certainly see why the Kids might have wanted to get the fuck out of Dodge. Plus, I had challenged that dark entity to a drunken duel, so it made sense that the Kids would see me as a protector of sorts. It definitely tracked that they came with me than that they were already here when I moved in. So in a sense I had sort of "adopted" some wayward spirits. Those little devil sprites seemed happy enough in our house that they were constantly driving me ape shit with their shenanigans. Ah well, so be it then—what am I going to do, complain? Call a fucking exterminator to spray for often-unseen ghost kids with a habit of book stacking? First I would be arrested. Then I would be committed. Only after all that shit would the laughter die down so I could hear people properly insulting me again.

I often wonder what would happen if I left the circle to find another house in Des Moines somewhere. Would those kids follow me again? Would they stay in the house on the circle because they are so used to it by now and there is no darkness to worry about? Or would they stay on the circle because now they were a part of a home that had good memories and there was nothing to fear in the form of malevolent spirits with terrible purposes? It is indeed a boggle. I have had other houses besides the one on the circle in different states, and there had been times when things had happened in those houses—miles from Des Moines—that were eerily the same as the goings-on I have transcribed herein. Now before you go off half-cocked (snicker) saying things like, "Are you suggesting that poltergeists migrate?," let me just cut you off with a very familiar "Not at all!" I am not trying to put forth the idea that ghosts can travel hundreds of miles just to be near the person their energy is infatuated with. I am not saying that.

But what if it were true?

Think about all those stories of dogs and cats that, after being accidentally forgotten or left behind with a neighbor, overcome vastly huge distances to be reunited with their owners. Picture Pickles, the family's pet hound, braving his way through rain, sleet, and highway pirates (those *bastard* highway pirates . . .) just to rejoin his family The Snoots in lovely Burbank. Granted, he was only in Reseda—but hell, I could not do it! Well, I could, but that is beside the point. My point really is that a dog or a cat runs completely on instinct, and yet they have an ability to find "home" in a way that I have never seen anything else like on earth. Is it because of doggie ESP? Or is it because these animals, after spending years with these families, have developed a spiritual bond that cannot be explained? And if dogs and cats can do it, why not ghosts? Ghosts are people too! Well, you know what I mean. Is it love? Maybe. I know a few ghosts that spend time around me that are not here because they hate me. Trust me, it is a big fucking responsibility to know that somewhere close by there are people you cherished in life surrounding you. Maybe love is a little more tangible than we, as advanced chimps, are willing to allow. It would explain how love turns to hate on a dime when push comes to brutal shove. As an emotion, it is the king of the mountain. I guess I am saying that maybe love is a conduit for the attraction every soul in the world is able to feel.

From the spiritual travel side of this discussion, look at something as cool and hotly contested as astral projection, the ability to leave your body and surf the winds of the world using only your will to navigate and, consequently, bring you home when the journey is over. Thanks to the 1970s and miles upon miles of website source material, astral projection has become a phenomenon all its own, from free-wheeling hippies expounding about trips to places like Mars and Phoenix, Arizona (which, let's be honest, could totally be the same place when you have eaten enough magic mushrooms), to theoretical physicists explaining at length how their studies have shown promising evidence that astral projection could be plausible. Indeed, I stood on the shoulders of these giants when I was putting together the examples for my intelligent energy hypothesis. The idea I am attempting to stick on the proverbial wall is not so much its reality as it is a cause for pause and reasonable doubt. I am confining my thoughts to conjecture only in order to make sense of my original question: if I was in one of my other houses in a different state entirely, would it be possible for the Kids on the Circle to pay me a visit?

Well, let's look at the "facts," shall we? We have established that a savvy canine can cross great distances to get back to its emotional "home"—that being the human owners who take care of it. Also, we have taken a few seconds to accept the idea that astral projection is an ideal alternative to air travel (at least you do not have to take your shoes off to go through security). So if the Kids are indeed attached to me emotionally and they know I am in a certain location for a prolonged period of time, could their energies make the journey to wherever I am? Has there ever been a case of long-distance haunting? Am I just full of shit and babbling like a shaven baboon high on crystal meth? I concur that the last statement may totally be true even out of the context of the original conundrum. But it is an interesting idea. What if the attraction of the soul is so powerful that a smitten spook crosses great distances to be with the soul or souls it craves? That is assuming that something like distance is relevant. There was a posit—by a scientist of such high caliber I never bothered to look up his name—that instead of billions upon billions upon billions of electrons running through our bodies and the google plex of worlds around us, there is actually only one real electron in the universe, and that superelectron was so charged that it raced back and forth in infinity, through space and the galaxies and indeed through the very fabric of time itself. If that were true—that there is only one electron connecting all of us—then a distance of miles is a matter of thought, and nearly simultaneously you could be in that other place because it is essentially the same spot from a scientific point of view. In other words, the Kids could blink and go from Iowa to our house in Vegas.

I can actually *hear* you all tearing your heads off and kicking them into your yards. Sorry . . . actually no, I am not.

Before you all get suicidal, put down your guns, ropes, pills, and exhaust pipes. Remember: I am just a lowly singer who cannot be trusted with money, the remote control, or sharp objects. I just put thoughts together, which almost always gets me into trouble. I am the same guy who in high school had the very nifty yet lethal idea that a combination of Nair and pudding would make me millions. So pay more attention to my stories than to my slightly educated guesses. At least if you do that, you and I will keep all of our fingers, toes, and lower lips. But I am still convinced the Nair/pudding thing would have made me a fortune. It sells itself: women use Nair and everyone loves pudding. How the fuck could that go wrong? THEY CALLED ME CRAZY AS WELL! WELL, WHO IS CRAZY NOW, YOU JUDGMENTAL FUCK WITS? HAHAHAHAHA . . .

I went off again . . .

I have now lived on the Circle for over seven years. It is quiet, it is quaint, it is fairly secluded, and my neighbors really never bother me. Okay, except for the guy who lives down the street and on the corner—he once held my broom hostage and sent me a picture of it with that day's newspaper. There was also a note that said, "If you ever want to see your broom alive again, please sign these Slipknot T-shirts . . ." Come to think of it, maybe my neighbors are a little more bizarre than I give them credit. When I moved in I received—not in this order and not all from the same neighbor—cookies, brownies, rum, gin, and a six pack of PBR tall boys. So my cul-de-sac is a bit more bent than I am able to understand. However, this is less about my surroundings and more about the house itself. It is unassuming, has nothing in the way of secret rooms or a skywalk, and does not glow in the dark.

The yard is not massive, and the garage is not anything special. It is white with white trim—I can only imagine its embarrassment after May Day.

My house on the Circle is not a manor house. Hell, it is not even a prestigious purchase like a country home or a houseboat. It is not a mansion by any means, not even if you squint into rose-colored glasses after a tab of acid. It could blend in with any Sears catalog on earth. What it is can be summed up in a variety of seemingly inane but seriously important adjectives: comfortable, warm, nice, distinct, special, lived in, cozy, manageable, woody (yes, woody—fuck off), and thoroughly enjoyable to come home to when all is said and done. Surely, it is not a compound or a century-old colonial work of majestic architecture. It is not antiquated, and yet it is not very modern either. But you know what it is? It is a *home*. It welcomes those who have lived there before and those who are just visiting with the same amount of muted exuberance that you would get from the house you grew up in or your grandmother's house over Thanksgiving, Christmas, or Easter weekend. If this house had arms, it would hug you upon your return and squeeze you with a warm good-bye when it is time to leave. Quite frankly, it is truly the only home I have ever really known. Even my Gram's house, where I basically grew up, did not fill me with that sense of safety and contentment that this house has given me for so long now. Yes, it is plain and nondescript and from the outside looks as exciting as a bucket of brown sauce. But it is our family home. That is something a lot of people cannot brag about truthfully on any level. The fact that there is some sort of activity going on there is just frosting on the cake.

So my Kids on the Circle run this mediocre haven whether I am there to bedevil or not. I assume they get excited when we get home, but who knows—maybe they come visit us while we are gone and we just never notice them. Perhaps there is enough of that warm wonderful energy left in our wake to keep them happy in our absence, like leaving a bowl of food for the dog when you go on vacation. I would like to think that with all the fantastic memories we have had in that house, there is a residual presence of love in those walls, those halls, and the air itself. When you take the time to make a place special, it definitely shows. The overall feel of a place like that will make you glow and allow you to relax just for a second before you plunge back into this Darwinian madness we call planet Earth. It is important to have these places, throughout the world. Forget about the fittest for a second and remember that life is not just about surviving—it is about Life with a capital L. When you play Tag or Hide and Seek, there has to be Base. You race toward it with joyous panic and fervor, reaching out with the nails on your fingertips just to make contact before you are picked off by the prick who's It. When your skin grazes the surface, you scream out, "SAFE!" with buoyant excitement. The rules say you cannot stay on Base for the whole game, but you can until you catch your breath. Then you charge back into the game with a vengeance until the pursuit chases you toward Base again.

Sounds a lot like home, right? At least, it sounds like a good home.

I spent a lot of time making sure that house felt like anyone could come and hang out there, that everyone good was welcome, and anyone with shitty intentions should just keep on fucking walking by. It is one of those precious things in my life that I do my very best to take care of, to keep whole. My wife and I are constantly working, and yet we know we have that place, that sanctum sanctorum to fall back to when the war of life gets a little too hairy. If those "kids" want to call it home too, what kind of a prick cocksucker would I be to deny that? It is my belief that everyone should have a touchstone to cling to when life starts to kick your ass and push you toward the cliff. It should be one of those inalienable rights we go on and on about as Americans. If we cannot have at least that, what is the point of all this? If there is time to go shopping for frivolous belongings, there is time to set the foundation. If there is time to download apps and stolen music, there is time to build the walls. If there is time to devote to booze and drugs and bullshit, there is time to seal the roof and bless it with a little bit of the soul. I put the time in, and the proof is there for all (who are invited) to see. With the Kids on the Circle there to raise hell, run amok, and keep me on all ten of my toes—even the broken one, Hugo—it seems like there is just a little bit more soul there than I had planned on in the beginning. But all plans are made to fail if you never allow room for the unexpected. I guess I must have, because those kids are welcome. At this point they are family.

And family is what makes a home.

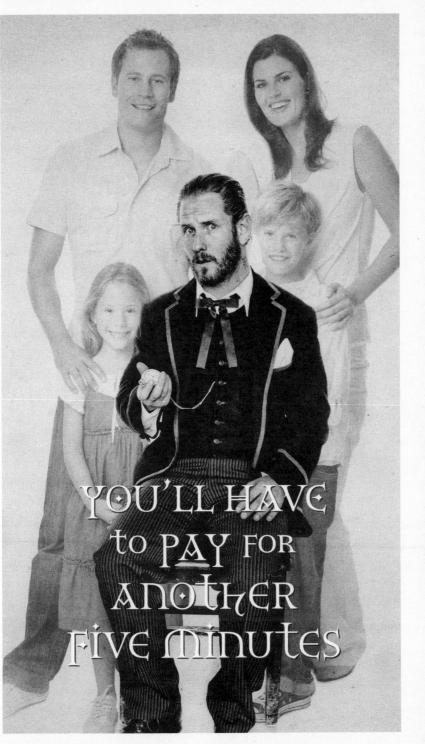

F RIENDS, ROMANS, COUNTRYMEN, lend me your ears, because it is time to do that groovy shake known as "sum it all up, Batman."

As you may recall, in my first book I talked about some time I spent in a gnarly little farmhouse just outside of Dewar, Iowa, when I was twelve years old. We lived there during the fall/winter. Everything around the place was essentially dead or dying. Set bleakly against a decaying gray sky with temperatures that dropped even lower when the ferocious wind was threatening to blow us away, the house was like living in my own personal horror movie. The nearest neighbor was miles down the crusty gravel road, so signs of life were scarce to none around this barren place. Just to be able to see my friends from school I had to beg rides from my mother or my mother's none-too-thrilled best friends with whom we shared this creepy haunt. It was indeed a hard solstice; I was beginning to hate the world in the worst way. This was the same house you may remember where I lived in a fucking closet with no light, no electricity, and no heat. I hated the place. But I discovered something there that I will never forget.

It was in this house of horseshit that I first saw the original and thoroughly incredible *Night of the Living Dead.* There was a local late-night creature-feature show on Channel 6 that used to run old, crappy cult classics, ostensibly for the entertainment of a handful of college students who might be up "studying" at that hour. It was hosted by a vapid, balding, middle-aged hack dressed as a low-rent Dracula called "Count . . ." something or other—I cannot even remember the character's last name. I only know he was called Count something because he had a rap song he pressed onto vinyl that was twice as lame as he was. It made Dangerfield's song "Rappin' Rodney" sound like N.W.A. Half the time I did not even get the chance to see what was on—there was only one TV in the house, and that was usually dominated by our in-house alcoholics watching burned VHS tapes containing *Dirty Dancing* and *Look Who's Talking Too.* So this was a rare occasion: I was home, alone, and I could do whatever I wanted.

It was the night before Halloween, which was on a Saturday that year. My "guardians" were out because it was Friday, and why stay at home with the family when it was a Friday? My sister was staying overnight with a friend. I sat in the house, contemplating what I should do. I was, of course, out in the boonies with no adult supervision. Should I start a fire? Should I look for a gun? Should I get high? Should I drink a beer? These were all wonderfully obvious options for a twelve year-old boy. But in a foreshadowing of good judgment I would not possess again until my thirties, I finally settled on watching TV in peace for once. I pulled on the power button, and the twenty-inch tube beast fired up with a spark and a flash of white light streaking across the screen. It just happened to be on channel 6; the Count was giving some speech dripping with drivel and useless vaudeville throwaways, and I was just about to switch it to channel 3 and look for a video when he announced that night's feature: *Night of the Living Dead.* I had never seen it—hell, the only horror movies I had ever watched were the children of *Halloween,* like *Friday the 13th, Nightmare on Elm Street,* and a weird one called *Happy Birthday to Me,* which starred one of the girls from *The Waltons,* I think. This was something different. So I plopped on our secondhand couch, lit a stolen cigarette, and hunkered down for a nice, scary movie.

Needless to say, it fucking terrified me.

First of all, it was in black and white. Black-and-white films to me are much more scary; I do not know if it is the graininess that somehow gives it the feel of a documentary that actually happened or what, but I get supremely fucked up by black-and-white films. Second, the house where they eventually hole up looked *exactly* like the fucking house I was living in, so after an hour I was bouncing between watching the movie and looking out the windows for starving naked zombies feasting on victims or random bugs. By the time the film was over, I was so fucking scared I actually welcomed the presence of the drunken assholes as they arrived from a night at the bar—at least I was not in that damn house alone anymore. I headed up to my closet for bed. Needless to say, even with a house full of loud people, I was still unable to fall asleep very quickly. Every noise was a zombie invasion. Every voice seemed to be calling my name, hungry for brains and blood.

After a while I came to make peace with the house, the irony being that shortly after I did, we moved again anyway. But I had learned a valuable lesson in that time: sometimes there is nothing to be afraid of. Sometimes it is your imagination and nothing else. I figured out the hard way that it is the threats you can see that can do the most damage—and usually do. Because of that house, I stopped worrying about the things that were not in plain sight. Maybe that is one of the central themes for this book: stop stressing on the shit that has not happened. I know there are people living in houses that seem to have uninvited roommates, and those interlopers tend to keep them on edge. My advice to them is take back your house—do not be intimidated by the, shall we say, extracurricular activity. Do *not* hire an exorcist unless you enjoy the process of cleaning up incense and sage while also drying off the walls when they are covered in holy water. If that is your kink, fucking have at it. In fact, make the priest wear leather and a helmet to enhance the sense of drama. Go for broke: play the musical score from *Conan the Barbarian*—that will get you fucking pumped, and it is also about as useful as bringing in a well-dressed holy man with a canteen full of H_2O blessed in a glorified bird feeder where strangers dipped their grubby fingers.

The best thing to do is what I said before: take back your house. Walk around and yell—it is even more effective if you do it buck-ass nude. Throw your own stuff; it will confuse them as much as anything else, and at least when you break something, you know who did it. The main message is do not be afraid of them. You may experience some physical contact and you might even encounter a situation in which they try to hurt you. But my opinion is that it takes so much energy for them to make a fuss and so little for any of us to brush it off like nothing happened. You are going to have times when you are uneasy—that is natural. The creep level on a poltergeist is pretty high up there, and it is just plain unnatural for things to move on their own. But that moment is brief and fleeting; once it passes, life goes on just the way it did before the chandelier started swinging and blinking or the drinking glasses began pushing themselves out of the cabinets. Clean it up, throw it away, and move on—it is as simple as that. If you want to feel something, get pissed because now you need new glasses. However, be constructive with that wave of emotion and chastise them like children. It is an energy akin to children who do not know their own strength. Every once in a while you are going to have to clean up after them.

And as I said, there are better (or worse) things to be afraid of. Humans are notoriously atrocious to each other. I think you have a better threat of home invasion by real thugs than by ghostly ones, and that kind of violence leaves a mark that lasts longer than anything else on the planet. It is not like we live in the jungle and are surrounded by big cats. It is not like we live on the Great Barrier Reef and have to make it to land before the great whites swim up from underneath and chew the fuck out of us in a massive and spectacular breach. It is not like we sleep in a hammock at night and there is a chance a brown recluse spider could crawl on our face and make us necrotic with one fatal bite (well, no one reading *this* book anyway). The majority of the human rat race really just kind of rubs shoulders with . . . well, each other. There is the rare bolt of lightning and the occasional circus elephant rampage, but the only truly viable threat is the motherfucker next to you on the bus. Sorry—I know a lot of hippies and liberals want to ignore that idea and feel that if we all start drinking the same milkshakes, there will be world peace and renewable fuels and bullets that only chastise people. Life does not work that way—life only gives you the pieces. You have to put the puzzle together yourself.

I am not saying the next person you sit beside on the trolley is a serial killer either. I am simply making a point to the people who suffer unneeded paranoia and stress because of the haunts in their homes. What I am saying is that there are other things that deserve that kind of attention, and if you waste those emotions on things that do not really need it, you will not see the real shit coming until it is right in your face and unavoidable. Nightmares have enough fuel in the subconscious without throwing more lambs to your lions. This is your life, those are your things, and that is your fucking home. Dissipate their power and mend. So they come back—who gives a wet runny shit? Do it again, and again, and again until it quiets down. Their sense of "daily chores" is about as innocuous as a mouse fart on Sunday. There is nothing they can do to you that is truly dangerous as long as you know they are there and you know it is coming. After that, it is as easy as being calm and taking names.

I knew the risks when I started writing this book. I knew how people would regard a whole tome about this crazy person who sees and reacts to ghosts. But this is the great part about being me—I do not give a flying fuck what people think about me. You show me an expert who knows all the answers, and I will show you a man who closes his store down before he has made any money. You can believe whatever you want. You can even expound at length about how these "beings" do not and will never exist. It does not change the fact that I have had these experiences. If you are going to call me a liar, step to my face and do it. If not, shut the fuck up. I am not saying there is no merit in any of their arguments. As a man who puts no stock in God and his Sunshine Band, I do not blame them for a second. But I deserve the same in return: you were not there and you are not me. I may go on about religion, but I do not condemn the people who use the practice in their lives the way it was intended. I have wonderful friends who are Christians, like my friends in the band Skillet, and they are some of the best people I have ever met. I only really crack off when people commit hell in heaven's name. The others are safe from my brutality. I do my best not to make sweeping statements so I do not get swept up in hype and hypocrisy. I also do not rail against the other end of the carpool, the ones who do not subscribe to anything that has not been proven or at least warrants a special on the Discovery Channel. All I say is that this is my story and this is what I have seen and been through. This book is for sharing, helping, and exploring—nothing more.

When it comes to what these spirits are and why they are around in the first place, religious doctrine gives few answers that really give me satisfaction. Maybe that is my own bias getting in the way of embracing their side of the fence, but I doubt it. Catholics and the like have their rituals to deal with the phenomena, and yet it never seems to do any good. Plus, there is no practicality about it; a house swarming with invisible rascals does not even register if you throw some suds around and light some candles. They may enjoy the prayers and the attention, but who knows? Almost every testimony of ghostly confrontation that I have heard or read about that includes an exorcism has revealed that it never solved the problem, and the family is left helpless and eventually moves away. Man, FUCK THAT! When you apply a more realistic approach to the issues, it may not stop these things from happening, but at least it gives you a sense of propriety, that this house is yours and no one is going to drive you from it, *ever*. It takes time and application, but it builds that peace that only the strong can understand. You have to be strong in the face of fear; it is the only way to leave that indelible mark on what is yours in life.

On the flip side, the scientific and generally pragmatic communities really just disregard any mention of anything as fantastic as ghosts and hauntings, despite countless bits of evidence and stories to the obvious. The extent of their imagination consists of zeros and ones, theories and studies, white coats and black holes. They continue to look to the unexplored heavens or depths, concerned with proving their own ideas while disproving others, though these may have merit or none at all. The only comparison I can make is how most people who can afford to donate to charity choose to do so as far from their front doors as possible, while more pressing issues closer to home are ignored or disregarded. That is the way I see it anyway—I may be right or I may be wrong. But truth be told, I at least know the difference between conjecture and a statement that, in retrospect, may make you look like a fool. I refuse to believe that the universe is the last frontier where fabulous mysteries reside. This world is lucky enough to have developed in the first place, through a collision of meteors, water, and wayward bacteria. Who is to say this planet, with all its beauty, has no capacity for the existence of the paranormal? Things like spooks and the like may be a part of the reason many of the "gods" and myths were created hundreds of years ago. There may well be explanations for everything I have said. Maybe I saw a human in Cold House. Maybe there was a person in the corn outside of Indianola. Maybe I was blown down the stairs on Foster. Maybe I was victim of mass hysteria at the Mansion. Maybe there was nothing in Farrar. Maybe my house on the Circle simply moves around and settles, like most houses its age eventually tend to do. Maybe all of this is nothing. Maybe . . .

Then again . . . maybe not.

What if I am onto something? God, could you imagine that? Could you imagine the looks on the faces of scientists, physicists, mathematicians, theorists, and geniuses around the world? They would pause, put down their chalk at the blackboard (because that is how I imagine all of them at any given time of the day), and quietly ask, "Are you telling me a brash, loud-mouthed heavy-metal singer with no actual training nor any discernible education put together a hypothesis about the existence of spirits and how it relates to energy . . . and it was *right*?" I can almost *hear* their heads exploding. I have been saying it since I threw a desk at my ninth-grade English teacher: be careful how you perceive the ones around you. Just because you are smart, that does not necessarily mean you are clever. The same people who crack the codes of the universe are still completely oblivious to how you keep brown stains out of white underwear. I figured that shit out in junior high school—simply refuse to wear underwear. But what do I know? I am just a brash, loud-mouthed heavy-metal singer and so on and so forth . . . .

Now, I am the kind of rabid bastard who immediately jumps to the extreme on things. So the possibility of me being right about these phenomena from a scientific point of view has me chasing dragons. I see myself accepting a Nobel Prize in science, getting the sash and the cash while flipping off the audience with my tongue sticking out. They could do a special on me for *Nova,* a wonderfully underrated, underappreciated program on PBS that I have watched for years now. I would book myself on the talk show circuit and say unbelievably inappropriate things like, "I wonder if Britney Spears smells funny . . ." simply because I fucking could. I would be the toast of towns around the world if my deductions were indeed plausible and provable. I would be the one-eyed man in the blind kingdom, kicking people in the ass when they were too slow in the buffet line and tripping the guys who made fun of me in high school. I would be emperor of all.

The problem is that when I think about that shit I am reminded all too often that I am no amazing scientist. Hell, I have to be reminded to put the fucking seat down in the bathroom (*one* soggy butt and I am an asshole for life . . .). So I am not trying to outdo Galileo or outwit Newton and his ilk. But crazier things have been possible. I am reminded of Srinivasa Ramanujan. Ramanujan was a self-taught mathematician from India who did almost all of his research in the middle of nowhere—he once applied to a college and failed because the only course he *passed* was mathematics. It was only after he submitted various papers to academics in England that his genius was really discovered and fully realized.

Ramanujan went on to revolutionize the medium, with break-throughs in mathematical analysis, infinite series, continued fractions, and number theory—all of this from a man who simply taught himself and unlocked the hidden power of his mind. Think about this: Ramanujan tragically died at the very young age of thirty-two. With all that he was able to achieve in the time he had, imagine if he had lived a longer life. Think of the possibilities. This is not a story of sadness; this is a story of inspiration, with a very simple message: the only limitations in life are the ones you conjure up for yourself and, thusly, then allow to control your destiny. Without those shackles, you can be invincible.

I fear again I may have failed my mission with this book. I wanted to examine instances in which the paranormal was a factor in my already loony life. I wanted to cast the twelve-sided die on the idea of God and deal with His supposed existence. I wanted to defend my position as an atheist and yet maybe make some sense of all these wonderfully amazing mysteries that seem to descend on my habitation with alarming frequency. I wanted to put forth different ideas that had nothing to do with superstition, myth, legend, religion, or mysticism to try to explain what these spirits, spooks, ghosts, and such could possibly be when we strip away the sitcom side of things. I do not know if I accomplished any of that. I am not even sure if I answered my own questions. Christ, did I invent *new* questions? At the end of the day, how far did I really go with all of this? Was I meant to know the truth, if there was any to know at all? In my quest for enthralled enlightenment, I may have left the safety of the street lamps and plunged a little too close to the alleys our parents warned us away from when we were young. But of course, no one learns anything sitting on the curb—you have to cross that street to really know what is on the other side.

I have been reading recently about several fascinating studies that are going on involving writing information—really truly encoding programmed knowledge—onto energy itself. Think of *that* for a second. Can you understand the ramifications of that idea? It has me thrilled and intrigued. The idea that we could eventually emboss light and energy with information—to possibly be able to control that energy with intelligence—is astonishingly exciting. Could you imagine sending messages on a beam of light? Not that stuff we use today, like fiber optics and whatnot, but using beams of pure energy for communication. It is one step removed from using that same energy for transportation. The laws of physics basically state that we, as not-so-durable humans, could not endure space travel physically. Okay, but what if the secret to long-distance space travel exists in the work I just described? And more in keeping with the theme of this damn book, what if this study, as a side-effect, proves my "intelligent energy" idea? If we as humans can write or encode energy with information—more to the point, somehow program the very electrons that make up the universe—how is it not plausible that a soul (energy), over a vast period of time and with enough power of will and thought, might *imprint* on that energy its personality (information), and as a result, after the physical form has died, its soul can go on with all that knowledge for an incredible amount of time because energy can neither be created nor destroyed? The human body is equal parts organism, supercomputer, and high-powered battery. I refuse to believe, with all these pieces and all these clues, it is *that* far-fetched to assume that this may not be possible. I am not trying to convince myself of anything; I have "seen the footage," so to speak. I may be trying to convince you that what I am saying has gravitas, but at least I am not cribbing notes from a shitty horror movie.

However, that leads me to the other revelation that I had as I was writing this book and putting this all in place. So assume for a moment that this idea of programming energy is a realistic endeavor. By all accounts and from what I have read, the progress has been slow but promising. So if we accept that as a viable component to this next equation, doing so makes this next set of ideas very interesting, even for a cynical bastard like myself. Let me explain: there have been other studies conducted that have looked at the world from the standpoint that planet Earth—from the seas to the air, from the country to the cities (yes, the cities), from the rock foundations to the humans who scamper across its face like "cells"—planet Earth might just be considered a superorganism. Yes, that is right: Earth, if you look at it as a whole, might be considered a single living being that just happens to have several species and communities clinging to it and shaping the way it "lives." If you think about it, it is not so crazy. Cities, with all their traffic, progress, and citizens, are not that far off from how human cells work or how organs pump blood and various fluids through the body, keeping us alive. What if everyone on this planet was keeping Earth alive in the way that our assembled cells, bacteria, fluids, and energies keep us alive? Physicist Jürgen Schmidhuber says the same pattern works on an intergalactic scale as well, from galaxies to universes. It is indeed an awesome idea.

So my idea is this: what if all the energy in the known universe and beyond, way beyond and even further, was connected? If we can write information on energy, it stands to reason that there may be a way for energy to commingle and cross itself without dissecting itself. We know we can store energy and we know we can harness energy. We are on the verge of using pure energy as a communication tool. So what if all that energy is not different—it is just parts of the same "being"? Moreover, if that incredibly humongous amount of energy is the same . . . what if that being were "God"? Yeah, I told you it was going to get weird—I even surprised myself on that one. I am not proving the existence of Old Man White Beard or rewriting the modern Bible; I am just making a suggestion. What if all that energy was not bits of different energy but instead a singular intergalactic supreme energy that runs not only this world but also *all* the other worlds and beyond? Would that energy not trigger the semiprimitive intuitions in the Neanderthal compartments of our brains that cause us to want to pray and believe in "a higher power"? It may be this unconscious perception that fuels our belief systems when it comes to religious fervor and the like. We have always been *surrounded* by fields of energy—we have been since we monkeys started talking, even before we "discovered" electricity and all that jazz. Our genes are enriched with diabolical wonder for answers and hyperinstinct, whether it is a preternatural sense of danger from predators or a curiosity about the invisible connections that draw us in, leave us baffled, and ultimately promote us to explain it all or see it all for what it truly is. Maybe since before the age of reason we have known that there is one immense power in the universe, and our limited understanding translated that into a God variable. It begs the quandary: if we can literally control and program energy, what if someone else already has? What if we are receiving subliminal ideas from the energy around us that originated somewhere else entirely, and we are only now starting to comprehend the capacities? What if our discoveries are not our own? What if our knowledge came to us on preprogrammed light?

This is usually the time in the TV show when the voiceover would announce dramatically that "ancient astronaut theorists believe" blah fucking blah and all that. I know—I just stepped deep into the realms of fringe science and "holy hell, what the pure fuck is he babbling about?" I embrace the fact that many of you might not follow these strings of patchwork postulation. I might just be typing fancy-looking words onto paper in an attempt to look a little less stupid than I did when I broke my toe running up a flight of concrete stairs. I am not saying it all makes sense, and I am not saying I have any answers past what I just put together here for you. What I am saying is, "I do not know, but it *could* be this . . ." Maybe that is the sign of terrific intellectual hunger. Maybe it is the sign of a lazy sod who does not bother reading what has already been established in academics. But you do not find unknown locations by taking the same bus with the same passengers to the same old stops. You grab a big stick, whack at the tall grass, and make your way in the direction of the place you believe is out there. It might not make sense to everyone around you, but at least when you get there you can describe it to the people you left behind.

I have been fairly obsessed with trying to understand ghosts and haunts from a very different point of view since I could string sentences together. It is the same reason I dismissed religion when I was younger: I was not satisfied with the answers that the status quo had to offer. That applies here because I am not completely sated by what the various ghost-hunting outfits could provide. Most of them I really just dismiss out of hand anyway. They are one weird decision away from being at a Renaissance Fair, and that to me is not what this is supposed to be about. This is not about Live Action Role Playing, and I am not saying there is anything wrong with that at all. But when you are truly looking for answers, you are not going to find any within a group who may or may not believe in what they are doing and most are secretly only doing so in order to belong to a group. There is a time to play and a time to work (man, I wish more people honestly understood that). Subsequently, there is a time to guess and there is indeed a time to ask. Those two concepts are not the same. You have a better chance of reaching your destination by seeking directions than you do by bullshitting yourself into knowing where the fuck you are on the map.

In summation, class (sorry, I could not resist), this is a dissertation on knowing, believing, theory, hypothesis, and examination. I may not have changed any of your minds in doing so. I may have made some enemies in the long run (I *knew* I should have left out the L.A.R.P. comment . . .), but this to me has been so therapeutic for my hungry mind that I feel I have really figured some things out and put some things in their respective place. Trust me—I am not an idiot, but I am not an asshole either. These are not sweeping statements meant to allege that I may know more than I am letting on about. I am just like you, but with worse hair. I want to know certain answers if only to be able to figure out the right questions in the process. If I knew where to start, I would not be writing this book. Sometimes I feel like a guy who runs into a theater in the middle of the movie and, while the rest of the film is playing, starts screaming loudly about what he thought the first half was about. But unlike most dismissive blokes I have had the displeasure of chatting with, I have embraced the idea that I may have no fucking idea what I am going on about in the first place. That to me is the healthiest place to start, because at least then you know you are going to accept correction with a smile and not balk at being wrong with an unhealthy grimace. We cannot all be right; somebody has to be a stupid fucker sometimes. The great thing about the democracy of the human race is that everyone eventually gets to take his or her turn at being wrong.

I had an interesting conversation with a good friend of mine I will refer to as Grover. I was explaining to him the concept of this book and trying to relay what I wanted to accomplish with it. Grover listened intently, throwing in quips here and there on how he had spent some time in places that were purportedly haunted as well. But his ideas about it were even more interesting. He wondered if it had to do with time. What if time somehow was able to fold back on itself, and the spirits we ran into were flashes from lives already led in time, like a loop from a film or a tape recorder? It was an inspiring idea—I mean, space is curved and light can curve, why not time? I wanted to include it here because I would be disingenuous if I said it did not intrigue me. I love hearing other people's concepts because it spurs me on toward real insight. Whether Grover or I are actually right is neither here nor there. What is relevant is that people are thinking about it outside the norm, and that is what this book is inevitably meant to be: a conduit that prods the reader into thinking for him or herself. I dislike references that lay down the law and render the person a slave to what is being posited. I think the best tools are the ones that leave you wondering when you are finished. The best art has always been the art that is left open to interpretation. That is what I hope you have in your hands right now.

As the light wanes and the pictures are taken from the walls, as the evidence and composites are boxed up for posterity, the rooms go gray and gold again while the dust settles all around. There is silence now where there was loud contemplation and gestures of feigning madness. The coals from burning determination go cold and lose their glow. This is the aftermath of a campaign; this is where aspiration finds time to sleep off the dregs of the party. As I look over this work in progress, I understand a few things a little more clearly, but mostly I have more questions than I started with prior to the typing of the first sentence. I guess that was the point—after all, I am not so much trying to change the world as much as a few minds, including my own. It is a startling thing, change. It shoots through your arms and into your mind like a rocket of pure adrenaline. It is a jarring, violent sequence of conclusions and acceptance, hardwired understanding, lightning in a throttle. The problem with our species is that we all do not take kindly to strangers like change. It usually takes a few bouts with a shotgun and a lot of shouting "GET OFF OF MY LAWN!" before we stop to even consider the idea of taking it seriously. It takes conversations and compromises all over the known world before it eventually becomes a video on the Internet that is passed from e-mail to e-mail like a group of survivors splitting a Hershey Bar—a joyless sparring of self-preservation and self-sacrifice.

Hey, it could be worse. We could be talking about using flamethrowers to clean up our lawns or, worse yet, a set of nail clippers to cut down Sequoia trees in Northern California. These are not so much impossible as they are improbable. Maybe the idea that the paranormal has more of a basis in science than in superstition is indeed improbable. But I refuse to think that it is impossible. I think I did a pretty decent job at establishing reasonable doubt, your honor. Now let my people go. Ideas are so simply intricate that they can never be destroyed. They can be ridiculed and disassembled. They can be disrespected and reduced to trash sometimes. But they cannot be destroyed as long as the person who tosses it on the wind understands the obstacles and derision that may lie ahead. Thoughts like these have kept humanity driving forward for thousands of years, even if the road around us is lined with fingernail scratches because we went there unwillingly. Still, I am not an innovator, just a facilitator. In my hands are the spores and seeds of a foreign organism. All it will take to unleash it into your minds is one strong exhale. So I will fill my lungs with air and smoke, and I will blow your minds, whether you like it or not.

I hope you enjoyed my tales of wonder. I promise I did not make these up. It has been a dark privilege to carry these over the years, collecting more as life has flown by, and I provided them here with relish for your entertainment. I also hope you appreciate the crazy attempts at conjecture; it is not every day a kid from the south side of Des Moines, Iowa, gets to emulate a theorist of sorts. It was hard and ate up a lot of time, but it was also fun and fascinating and I shall definitely do it again. In addition, I pray (no pun intended) I did not offend you with my rather withered and bitter sentiments about organized religion. I have no qualms about faith, just the people who try to control it. They have no right to control things like that because it is every person's right to believe what they want. Too many cooks spoil the soup, and too many kooks spoil the soul. Faith, when all is said and done, should be an independent journey for the person with the questions. It should not be a racetrack where the guy who owns it gets to tell you where you are going to go. No one should control the way of faith except the one who is doing the praying. Everyone outside that particular circle should disavow themselves, and the pun is *definitely* intended there.

I have my answers. I have my questions. I have a bit of borrowed time on my hands. I have my lucky corduroys on as well as my *Doctor Who* jacket and a fresh charge in my Ion eCigarette (yeah, I quit smoking while I was writing this book). I guess it is time to put the hood down on the supercharged cruiser and head back onto the highway for now. I promise it will not be for long— I know I will come up with another insane concept for another book soon enough. It might be a bit, but I know me—I have an infuriating lack of control over how my brain works, and when a tirade or rant comes on, there is no fucking stopping it. Half the time I am left hoping it can restrain itself long enough to let me get a little sleep. But the fucker is *consumed* with Mötley Crüe's *Too Fast for Love* right now. Every night I am just on the verge of nodding off, and all of a sudden it is the opening riff to "Live Wire" raging in my subconscious. Hey, I do not blame it—that is a great fucking song. But at 3 A.M. it can be a little annoying.

As I move on out of sight, let me remind you: believe what you want, but try not to forget what you know in the process. Belief is a gift you should cherish; knowledge is a gift you should never squander. I see it all the time: the glazed eyes of the believer blatantly casting undue doubt on something as wonderful and freeing as a fact. This simply cannot stand. This is not the way to the future. This is how you end up broke, fucked, and crazy. If there is a God, there will be time enough to meet him. If there is no God, shit happens and get on with your life. The world is full of things to believe in and embrace, like charity for others and justice for the afflicted, food for the hungry and love for the hated. If you need to incorporate these into your religious programming, then do it. But do not render these beneath you because of "God's Plan." We as humans can actually *do something about it*. Religion should never be a crutch; it should be an operation that lets you walk on your own again.

I believe in the paranormal. I also know from past experience that these things exist. I believe these things are a part of something I call "intelligent energy," which combines the powers of the soul and mind and encodes the energy of that soul with information, and thereby the longevity of that energy is made remarkable with personality and action. I have a pretty good idea that this is true because of the stories I have provided in this book. Take them or leave them; challenge them or accept them. Just do not dismiss them because of their context. Do not sneer at these ideas and stories just because they do not fit into your established take on what this world has to offer. Some people think very little of the world and most of the animals and plants that call it home. I am defiantly *not* one of those people.

I look forward to the debates. I look forward to the dismay. Shit, I even look forward to the out and out anger this book of mine might provoke. But in my opinion if you are not contributing to the conversation, you do not automatically reserve the right to speak. I want minds ready for fire and flame. There is no shame in ignorance as long as you do not try to hide behind it. For me the conversation begins now. It begins with this book. It will continue long after I have finished writing it. It will go on hopefully after I am gone. Maybe I will come back. I know some of my friends and family have. But I do not run. I do not scream. I just wonder.

I JUST WONDER.

acknowledgments

As always, I could not have made this book a reality without the following list of enabling miscreants: Ben Schafer and all the wonderful people at Da Capo Press as well as Perseus Books for their continued belief in me and my shoddy abilities—and also for the leeway I received on the deadline; my agent, Marc Gerald, for being my spiritual cheerleader and getting me where I am in the book world; Paul Brown, Matt Kenny, and Stubs & Kirby for taking the time, making the effort, and going above and beyond for the artwork and the photos (still can't believe you got *that* outfit, Paul!); Cory Brennan and everyone at 5B Management— Bob, Kim, Diony, and Harold—you guys have no idea what kind of monster you're creating in me; Rob Shore, the keeper of the gates ("I'm Rob . . .") and all my friends at RSA; again, my ever-growing family: the Taylors, Bonnicis, Mays, and Bennetts, whose never-wavering trust is something that makes my foundations unbreakable; and finally, my wife, Stephanie—The Boss—who I will never be able to thank enough or truly convey to her just how special and invaluable she is to me.

ABOUT THE AUTHOR

Corey Taylor is the lead singer of both Slipknot and Stone Sour, and the author of the *Sunday Times* bestseller *Seven Deadly Sins*. A native of Des Moines, Iowa, he spends his time between there and the rest of the world.

www.thecoreytaylor.com